TEACHER STATUS AND
PROFESSIONAL
LEARNING

The Place Model

Critical Guides for
Teacher Educators

You might also like the following books from Critical Publishing.

Beginning Teachers' Learning: Making Experience Count
Katharine Burn, Hazel Hagger and Trevor Mutton
978-1-910391-17-4

Developing Creative and Critical Educational Practitioners
Victoria Door
978-1-909682-37-5

Developing Outstanding Practice in School-based Teacher Education
Edited by Kim Jones and Elizabeth White
978-1-909682-41-2

Dial M for Mentor: Critical Reflections on Mentoring for Coaches, Educators and Trainers
Jonathan Gravells and Susan Wallace
978-1-909330-00-9

How do Expert Primary Classteachers Really Work? A Critical Guide for Teachers, Headteachers and Teacher Educators
Tony Eaude
978-1-909330-01-6

Non-directive Coaching: Attitudes, Approaches and Applications
Bob Thomson
978-1-909330-57-3

Theories of Professional Learning
Carey Philpott
978-1-909682-33-7

Most of our titles are also available in a range of electronic formats. To order please go to our website www.criticalpublishing.com or contact our distributor, NBN International, 10 Thornbury Road, Plymouth PL6 7PP, telephone 01752 202301 or email orders@nbninternational.com.

TEACHER STATUS AND
PROFESSIONAL
LEARNING

The Place Model

Series Editor: Ian Menter

Critical Guides for
Teacher Educators

Linda Clarke

First published in 2016 by Critical Publishing Ltd

British Library Cataloguing in Publication Data
A CIP record for this book is available from the British Library

ISBN: 978-1-910391-46-4

This book is also available in the following e-book formats:
MOBI: 978-1-910391-47-1
EPUB: 978-1-910391-48-8
Adobe e-book reader: 978-1-910391-49-5

Cover and text design by Greensplash Limited
Project Management by Out of House Publishing
Printed and bound in Great Britain by 4edge Limited, Essex
on FSC approved paper

Critical Publishing
152 Chester Road
Northwich
CW8 4AL

www.criticalpublishing.com

CONTENTS

ABOUT THE **SERIES EDITOR**

Ian Menter is Emeritus Professor of Teacher Education and was formerly the Director of Professional Programmes at the University of Oxford. He previously worked at the Universities of Glasgow, the West of Scotland, London Metropolitan, the West of England and Gloucestershire. Before that, he was a primary school teacher in Bristol, England. His work has widely been published in academic journals.

ABOUT THE **AUTHOR**

 **Linda Clarke** was a geography teacher and head of department in public and private sector, selective and non-selective schools in England and in Northern Ireland for 15 years. On completing her Masters, she became an academic and teacher educator at Ulster University, gained a PhD and completed a term as head of the School of Education, before escaping back to her true delight in working with schools and student teachers. She was awarded a personal chair in 2012. Her research interests include teacher education, education technology and international development.

FOREWORD

It has become something of a cliché to say that those of us involved in teacher education *live in interesting times*. However, such has been the rate of change in many aspects of teacher education in many parts of the world over recent years that this does actually need to be recognised. Because of the global interest in the quality of teaching and the recognition that teacher learning and the development of teachers play a crucial part in this, politicians and policymakers have shown increasing interest in the nature of teacher preparation. Early in 2013, the British Educational Research Association (BERA) in collaboration with the Royal Society for the Arts (RSA) established an inquiry into the relationship between research and teacher education. The final report from this inquiry was published in 2014 and sets out a range of findings that include a call to all of those involved – policymakers, practitioners, researchers – '*to exercise leadership amongst their members and partners in promoting the use of evidence, enquiry and evaluation to prioritise the role of research and to make time and resources available for research engagement*' (BERA-RSA, 2014, p 27). One key purpose of this series – *Critical Guides for Teacher Educators* – is to provide a resource that will facilitate a concerted move in this direction. The series aims to offer insights for all those with responsibilities in our field to support their critical engagement with practice and policy through the use of evidence based on research and on experience.

This particular volume introduces a highly original and provocative way of understanding the nature of teaching and teacher education. In her Place Model, Professor Linda Clarke sets out a geographically and sociologically informed approach to questions about the relationship between teaching, teachers and society. She introduced this Model in her professorial lecture at Ulster University and has developed it very clearly in this volume. What her Model does is to raise questions of national and international significance about the ways in which teachers are positioned in societies and the enormous responsibilities that they shoulder, not only for the well-being and education of individual children with whom they engage but, more broadly, for the safety and development of communities and societies. Her work is informed not only by a long-standing involvement in teacher education in the UK (she contributed to an analysis of policy and practice across the UK and Ireland; see TEG, 2015) but also by her work in Sub-Saharan Africa, Malawi in particular.

Throughout the book, there are many critical questions that teacher educators will want to discuss with the beginning teachers they are working with, and there is also an outline plan for a workshop that will enable participants to understand more deeply the broader significance of their work as teacher educators and as teachers.

Ian Menter, Series Editor

Formerly Professor of Teacher Education, University of Oxford

February 2016

ACKNOWLEDGEMENTS

I would like to dedicate this book to my parents, Peggy and Francis Mackin, who believed firmly in the value of learning. I dedicate it, too, to my wonderful husband, Peter, and also to my equally wonderful children, Alice and Stephen, who seem to have the luxury of taking the learning-status nexus for granted in a way that I never could. I would also like to thank Dr Lesley Abbott who has been a thorough proofreader and a wise and kind adviser.

Linda Clarke

The Place Model

Who is teaching me today?

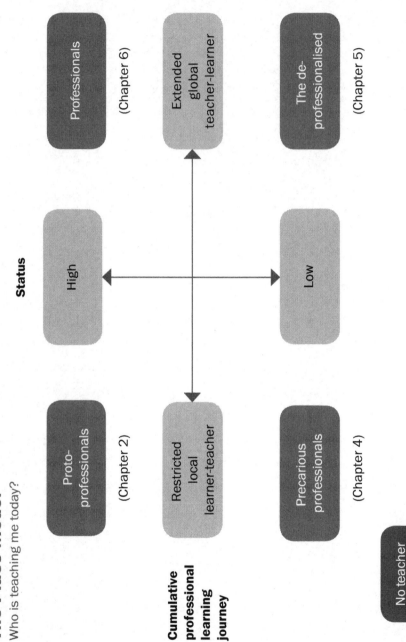

CRITICAL **ISSUES**

- *Why is teacher status important?*
- *Is there a relationship between teacher status and teacher professional learning?*
- *Why is the teaching profession often more criticised than it is admired?*

Introduction

Today a distinctive combination of good and bad news about status and professionalism goes right to the heart of the active review and development of teacher education across the UK and in many other countries too. The good news is that there is increasing recognition that *'the quality of an education system cannot exceed the quality of its teachers and principals'* (OECD, 2011, p 235). This international agreement coexists with the bad news: as William Louden, the Australian teacher educator, puts it, the bad news is *'the 101 damnations'* (2009) – the persistent blaming and shaming of teacher educators coupled with the notoriety of so-called *failing schools* and, indeed, *failing* teachers and principals. This public flagellation may be seen as a reflection of a perennial issue which is well expressed by Pam Grossman of Stamford: *'One of the challenges faced by efforts to gain professional status for teachers is that teaching is complex work that looks deceptively simple'* (Grossman et al, 2009, p 273). More disturbingly, it may be a product of the *'sticks, stones and ideology'* (Cochran-Smith and Fries, 2001) or the *'discourses of derision'* (Kenway, 1990) which are used by politicians to create *'rhetorical spaces within which to articulate reform'* (Ball, 2013, p 104). These reforms in the teaching profession are developing particularly rapidly in England and are widely recognised as part of a wider change agenda which is altering the status and skill sets of *The Twenty-First Century Public Servant* (Needham and Mangan 2013). Student teachers who will live out their careers within this perceptual maelstrom need to be given an early opportunity to deconstruct and contemplate the place of their profession. Teacher educators can support them to make a realistic yet ambitious analysis and to plan and build their own cumulative, career-long professional learning process that will take them from a learner-teacher to a teacher-learner while integrating local, situated knowledge with global expertise. This book presents a model, the Place Model, which provides a framework for that analysis. The Appendix offers a resource base for using the Place Model in a discursive workshop with student teachers.

The Place Model

The *Place Model* allows every teacher, from the least to the most experienced, to locate themselves within a metaphorical professional landscape and to compare their situation with that of all other teachers – everywhere, living and dead, fictional and real. In this model, two senses of *place* provide comparative lenses for a timely a priori examination of the place of the teacher:

1. place in the sociological sense of hierarchical status;

2. and also place in the humanistic geography tradition of place as a cumulative process of professional learning within ever-expanding horizons.

This chapter introduces the Place Model in the form of a visual representation, a map which provides a range of answers to the learners' question, *Who is teaching me today?* While the model takes the form of a map which resembles a *graph*, it is intended to be schematic or diagrammatic rather than mathematical in nature. Like all maps, it is subjective. Across the chapters of the book, a critical animation of this comparison is achieved by *populating* the Place Model with examples drawn from a range of sources and scales. These examples also permit you to consider how the Place Model can be used to map both career-long professional learning trajectories and to inform comparisons at individual and systemic levels.

The Place Model
Who is teaching me today?

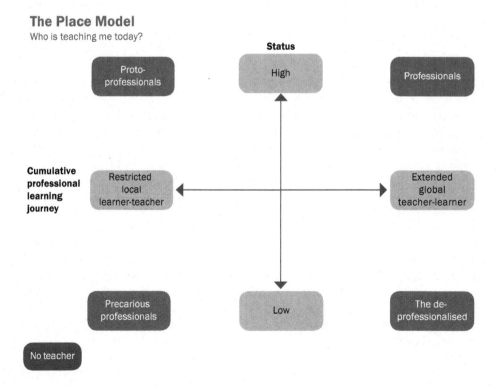

2

It is easy to forget that the learners, not their teachers, are the principal reason why the status and professional development journeys of teachers are so important. Learners are entitled to be taught by high-status teachers for whom continuing professional development (CPD) is a cumulative, career-long journey, so the sub-heading of the Place Model asks the question, on behalf of learners everywhere, *Who is teaching me today?* The answers to this question include local heroes, dragons, bullies, consummate professionals, you the reader and every one of your student teachers. Before exploring these answers, the two *axes* of the model are explained more fully.

Teacher status and professional learning: correlation or paradox?

The importance of this combination of status and professional learning journey was underscored by Eric Hoyle (1983) and has been recently echoed by Pasi Sahlberg (2012) in his explication of the widely acclaimed success of the Finnish education system. Sahlberg highlights, inter alia, two factors which are key strengths of teacher education in Finland: the status of teachers and the professional learning of teachers, as reflected in oversubscribed and ubiquitous Masters-level entry to the profession.

This very same pairing goes to the heart of teacher professionalism, as recognised by Eric Hoyle, writing in the year in which this author became a teacher, who described teachers as seeking a professionalisation which has two components:

» *the improvement of status*

» *the improvement of skills*

(1983, p 45)

However, while Sahlberg sees these two elements as interwoven and essential, Hoyle saw them as very much interrelated but paradoxical, for while teaching, he said, is seeking recognition of status as a profession, the types of professional development which are being undertaken will not advance professionalisation in the conventional sense, which is derived from occupations such as medicine or law. He saw the sorts of practice-based, non-award-bearing CPD courses of the time as having too little theory and research and, therefore, as actively detracting from the status of teaching as a profession.

Contemporary debates suggest that there is as yet little agreement about these matters and also that these arguments still matter very much to the teaching profession, policymakers and individual teachers. The current contentious debates about the locus of initial teacher education (in the classroom or in the academy), about whether this process should be called initial teacher *education* or initial teacher *training*, about the philosophical position of teachers (craftworkers, technicists or *professionals* (Winch et al, 2013) or *deliverologists* (Pring, 2012)), or about the nature of teacher CPD (practice-based, research-informed, research-based, collaborative and so on), all have intersections with the relationship between teacher status and teachers' career-long professional learning journeys, which is at the heart of the Place Model.

Geographical imagination

The conceptualisation of the relationship between status and a cumulative, career-long professional learning journey which is embedded in the Place Model is derived from Hoyle's paradox and also from Sahlberg's assertion of the primacy of this pairing at the heart of the Finnish Model, as noted earlier. The Model is also based on the humanistic geography tradition's notion of *geographical imagination*, which asserts the importance of status and location in knowing one's place in the world. In fact, the Place Model might be seen as an example of geographical imagination, whereby we position ourselves within our world relative to others and to other places. The notion of geographical imagination is widely used but poorly defined. It is derived from the humanistic geography tradition, particularly the work of Doreen Massey, who viewed place as process (1991). Within the Place Model it is used in the sense of how teachers (individuals or in various collective groupings) view and construct their position in the world. According to Allen and Massey (1995), *Geographical Imagination* allows us to construct meaning in the world by allowing us to understand our place in the world through comprehending:

1. place at a variety of scales, from the local to the global and how they are connected and interdependent;

2. our personal and collective place in the world – in terms of both sociological status and identity (and our relationship to nature – not so relevant here).

Massey (1991) explores the ways in which the local and global are increasingly interlinked through processes of globalisation. Those teachers who seek to gain deeper understandings of their own particular contexts through developing wider understandings of what is known globally about education through collaborations and research might be seen to demonstrate a well-developed geographical imagination in respect of their professional learning.

In addition, the Place Model may be understood at various degrees of aggregation so that each and every teacher can be imagined as having a personal professional *place* where he/she *fits* at any given time, because each has a unique set of professional perspectives and trajectories (processes). On the other hand, the profession as a whole, or smaller groups of teachers who share many elements of status and professional learning, may share a similar position in relation to each of the *axes* of the Model.

The horizontal 'axis' and the vertical 'axis': career-long professional learning and teacher status

It is important to begin unpacking the nature of the horizontal and vertical *axes* of the Place Model by delineating what each is *not*. The horizontal axis, representing a career-long professional learning journey, is *not* a time scale – it is *not* a matter of passive survival for 30–40 years in the classroom, picking up a few tips and tricks about good teaching on the way. Rather, the cumulative, career-long professional learning process is conceived as a developing place and, it must be stressed, *not* a space, using the Chinese-American geographer Yi-Fu Tuan's cogent formula:

Place = Space + Meaning (Tuan, 1977).

The vertical axis, on the other hand, is *not* about remuneration, although this is often both an important component and a significant reflection of status. This is often reflected in protracted union-led battles about teachers' pay and is also evidenced in the recent much-debated row in Ireland around *employing* unemployed teachers for €50 per week on the national JobBridge internship scheme (*Irish Independent*, 2014).

So, what do the axes represent? While the vertical axis is based on public perceptions of esteem for teachers (discussed towards the end of this section), the horizontal axis also draws upon Hoyle's (2008) earlier heuristic model of *restricted* and *extend*ed professionality (discussed below) and on Wenger's (1998) accounts of *Educational Imagination*.

Wenger defines educational imagination within the context of developing identity though learning. The concept has strong resonance with geographical imagination, and together they may be seen to serve to create a cohesive and useful conceptualisation of the place of teachers, which forms the basis of the Place Model. Wenger recounts the story of two stonemasons who were asked what they were doing. One stonemason said he was cutting a stone to a perfectly square shape, and the second said he was building a cathedral. Both answers are accurate and both masons may have been good at cutting stones. However, their contrasting answers *reflect different relations to the world* and different *functions of the imagination* (Wenger, 1998, p 176). The Place Model incorporates all three components of educational imagination advocated by Wenger within the career-long learning journey of its horizontal axis:

Orientation: Educational imagination is about locating ourselves- getting a panoramic view of the landscape and our place in it. It is about other meanings, other places, other times. It is about direction and trajectories. In this sense, it is about identity formation as an expanding image of the world.

Reflection: Educational imagination is about looking at ourselves and our situations with new eyes. It is about taking a distance and seeing the obvious anew. It is about being aware of the multiple ways that we interpret our lives. In this sense it is about identity as self consciousness.

Exploration: Educational imagination is about not accepting things the way they are, about experimenting and exploring possibilities, reinventing the self, and in the process reinventing the world.

(Wenger, 1998, pp 272–73)

The Place Model, and its use by student teachers (and serving teachers) to consider their *place*, is about orientation, getting a panoramic view of position and trajectory. Likewise, it requires reflection and openness to reinventing the future as an individual and in the interests of the entire profession. This expansive, reflective and exploratory view of learning also has strong resonances with Hoyle's identification of two types of professionality. Hoyle contrasted the *restricted professionality* with what he saw as a more ideal (but rarely found) *extended professionality*:

a restricted professional was construed as a teacher for whom teaching was an intuitive activity, whose perspective was restricted to the classroom, who engaged little with wider professional reading or activities, relied on experience as a guide to success, and greatly valued classroom autonomy.

(Hoyle, 2008, p 291)

By contrast,

an extended professional was construed as a teacher for whom teaching was a rational activity, who sought to improve practice through reading and through engaging in continuous professional development, who was happily collegial, and who located classroom practice within a larger social framework.

(Hoyle, 2008, p 291)

Linda Evans has built on this work using the term *professionality orientation* to refer to individuals' locations on what she saw as an extended-restricted continuum (2008).

The Place Model's horizontal axis is based upon such a continuum – a cumulative, career-long professional learning journey with teachers moving along a restricted-extended trajectory and seeking to explore and extend their geographical and educational imaginations across their careers. There is one final and crucial point to be made about this axis, this journey: student teachers must, first and foremost, be disabused of any illusions they may have that their education system is either designed or equipped to turn them into the very best teacher they can be – they must construct this journey for themselves.

While it is important that teachers seek to exert their agency in respect of building their own learning trajectory, and they may well have some leeway in this, it is likely that they will have less agency in respect of the vertical axis, which depends on the exigencies of public opinion of teacher status.

Teacher status

There is some considerable agreement on the importance of teacher status. While teacher salary may be an important component and reflection of status, Sahlberg (2012, p 4) notes that in Finland the most *'talented, motivated and creative'* seek to become teachers, but that upon graduation salaries for Finnish teachers are only slightly above the national average and just above the OECD average. Sahlberg describes Finnish teachers as having very considerable public esteem, *'akin to physicians, lawyers or economists'* and *'driven by moral purpose rather than material interests and rewards'* (Sahlberg, 2012, p 2).

There is a range of ways in which teacher status may be assessed. The international comparison carried out for the *Global Teacher Status Index* uses the criteria shown below:

  » how teachers are respected in relation to other professions;

  » the social standing of teachers;

  » whether parents would encourage their children to be teachers;

» whether it is perceived that children respect their teachers;

» what people think teachers ought to be paid;

» whether people think teachers ought to be paid according to the performance of their pupils;

» the degree to which people trust their education system;

» how much teachers are trusted to deliver a good education to our children;

» whether teachers' unions have too much power.

The Varkey Foundation's website (the Foundation owns a chain of schools, mainly in the Middle East, and provides philanthropic funding for teacher education initiatives) contains a detailed report and interactive graphics which permit many fascinating comparisons. Their study, which involved in-depth opinion polling by Populus in 21 countries, evidenced very considerable international variation, showing, for example, that out of the 21 countries surveyed only in China did people see teachers as having an equal status with doctors. In the UK, by contrast, less than 5 per cent of people thought that teachers had an equivalent status (Dolton and Marcenaro-Gutierrez, 2013, p 4). In the UK, the largest longitudinal study of teacher status was conducted by Hargreaves and colleagues (2011) who sought the perspectives of people who come into close contact with teachers, including governors, parents and teaching assistants, as well as conducting a study of media coverage of teachers and education. Their findings suggested, inter alia, that about half (49 per cent in 2003 and 47 per cent in 2006) of the general public surveyed considered teaching an attractive career and that the status of teachers had declined over the four decades proceeding the study. Intriguingly, the study found that teachers were not overly concerned with status, a finding which contrasts with other studies and indeed with the OECD's 25-country survey on teacher recruitment and retention, which identified the need to improve the '*status and labour market competitiveness*' of the teaching profession as the first priority in its first level of policy implications (OECD, 2005, p 10). More crucially, the Global Teacher Status Index report indicates that:

It is not just actual teacher wages that relate to student outcomes, but what the public estimates or perceives to be a teacher's wage. In countries where the estimated or perceived view on teacher wages was higher, student outcomes were better.

(Dolton and Marcenaro-Gutierrez, 2013, p 22)

Such criteria arguably merit some consideration by student teachers from the outset (see Further reading). The Place Model requires users to apply a subjective estimation, and status in the Model is based on estimations of public perceptions of the esteem in which teachers are held, ranging from low to high.

Populating the Model

The Place Model maps a professional landscape in a way which is intended to be an heuristic, based on subjective conceptions of geographic and educational imaginations, rather than a positivist equation. It may be possible to develop positivist scales based on the status studies mentioned above and on a rigorous empirical assessment of teacher learning trajectories, so that the Place Model becomes a graph. However, for the purposes of this book, the Model is a somewhat less than objective framework that will help student teachers make sense of their professional landscape. To this end, the remaining chapters of this book are partly based on bringing the Model to life by populating it with teachers (fictional and real) as a *Living Graph* (Leat, 1998), a classroom thinking skills technique which hypothetically positions real (and fictional) people, flesh and bones, within graphs. This approach also challenges everyone who calls themselves a teacher to be able to locate both themselves and their career trajectory – and, indeed, the teacher education system in which they work – within the Place Model. They must also be able to justify that positioning.

The following chapters examine each of the quadrants of the Model with reference to salient theoretical considerations and to some very contentious issues which are scrutinised with respect to a populace of hypothetical exemplars. Chapter 2 examines low-medium status, restricted professionalism and considers whether some fictional teachers from Dickens and Goldsmith and the technicist and craftworking models of the early twenty-first century fit in this quadrant of the Model. Chapter 3 discusses the plight and potential of some very contrasting scenarios in which a learner has no teacher, and Chapter 4 considers whether any teacher, no matter how short term or unprofessional, is better than none. Chapter 5 will examine some contrasting causes and consequences of de-professionalisation, and Chapter 6, by contrast, will draw the examination of the Model to a close by expanding Hoyle's notion of extended professionalism in the light of more recent understandings of teacher professional learning which foreground critical reflective practice, research-informed teaching and the increasingly widespread emulation of the *Finnish model*. This model has been introduced in Ireland, in Portugal and parts of Australia and has recently been recommended in the report of the most recent review of teacher education in Northern Ireland (DEL, 2014). On the other hand, the expansion of school-based models of initial teacher education must also challenge teachers to ensure that their professional development journeys are not limited to the horizons of one or two schools only. This book prompts and supports a high-status, expansive professionalism in which confident teachers can inspire pupils to seek wider horizons while continuing to value their local contexts.

IN A **NUTSHELL**

This chapter outlines the Place Model as an alternative, original way in which both teacher educators and student teachers can begin to consider the singular importance of career-long learning in supporting and sustaining a high-status teaching profession. Those who aspire to become teachers are also challenged to proactively plan and create their own professional learning journey and to ensure that they value both local knowledge and global expertise.

REFLECTIONS ON **CRITICAL ISSUES**

Student teachers should be aware that they are soon to enter a profession which seems to receive both plaudits and brickbats in equal measure, despite the self-evident importance of having high-status, highly skilled and learned professionals teaching every learner, everywhere. They should be prepared to proactively plan to ensure that they can move from being learner-teachers to teacher-learners, continuing to seek the high-quality, challenging professional learning opportunities which combine local and global expertise.

Further reading

Dolton, P and Marcenaro-Gutierrez, O (2013) *Varkey GEMS Foundation Global Teacher Status Index*. London: Varkey Foundation. [online] Available at: www.varkeygemsfoundation.org/sites/default/files/documents/2013 GlobalTeacherStatusIndex.pdf (accessed 9 September 2015).

Hargreaves, L, Cunningham, M, Hansen, A, McIntyre, D and Oliver, C (2011) *The Status of Teachers and the Teaching Profession in England: Views from Inside and Outside the Profession*. Synthesis for The Final Report of the Teacher Status Project, Department for Education and Skills Research Report, No 831B. [online] Available at: www.academia.edu/515522/The_status_of_teachers_and_the_teaching_profession_in_England_Views_from_inside_and_outside_the_profession (accessed 9 September 2015).

CRITICAL **ISSUES**

- *Describe a perfect professional mentor.*
- *What is the relevance of craftworker and technicist modes of teaching? Are these compatible with being a professional?*
- *How relevant is the high-status* village statesman *(or local hero) in the teaching profession of the early twenty-first century? Are such teachers invaluable to their local community/schools/profession/learners? Alternatively, do they have a constricting influence, narrowing horizons and limiting learning opportunities?*

Introduction

It is in this quadrant of the Place Model (see page x) that many teachers take their first steps as learner-teachers on their cumulative, career-long professional learning journey, if they are teaching in a context where teachers enjoy average to high public esteem. The term proto-professionals has been coined here, emphasising the prefix *proto*, which is derived from the Greek *prōtos* (first) and *pro* (before), to indicate that this quadrant is home to those teachers in the first stages of their professional journey. This chapter begins with a brief consideration of these early steps, including the role of mentors and also a community of practice model of professional learning, before examining the key characteristics of proto-professionalism. Proto-professionals also include those who may have been teaching for much longer periods and may even have considerable status, but whose professional journey is, nonetheless, limited. This quadrant is the home of Hoyle's *restricted professionals*:

A restricted professional was construed as a teacher for whom teaching was an intuitive activity, whose perspective was restricted to the classroom, who engaged little with wider professional reading or activities, relied on experience as a guide to success, and greatly valued classroom autonomy.

(Hoyle, 2008, p 291)

The restricted teacher might today be deemed a craftworker, and if their practice is driven by the delivery ('deliverology'; Pring, 2012) of formulaic protocols, the approach might, additionally or alternatively, be described as technicist (Winch et al, 2013). These two modes of teaching are examined in the latter part of this chapter. You and your student teachers are asked to consider whether this quadrant is the only valid location for these types of teachers within the Place Model and to reflect on the reasons why teachers may remain in this location, even while developing high public esteem, perhaps even as *local heroes*. They might consider whether only the least skilled teachers belong here, and perhaps, too, in the not-so-distant future, robotised teachers (Chapter 3). Less controversially, the chapter develops these arguments by populating the Place Model with two fictional teachers before challenging you to consider if such roles have parallels today.

Beginning teachers and their mentors

These early steps in the teaching profession are often characterised as a period when students and beginning teachers are very narrowly focused on their own *performance* in the classroom at a specific time and place, rather than on their pupils' learning or on the future trajectory of their professional learning. Such a self-absorbed focus is, perhaps, understandable at a time when an inexperienced teacher is faced with numerous challenges within what Wragg (1974) called the '*intoxicating task of survival*'. In the best systems, it is also the time when the nascent teacher has access to the very finest professional support, usually in the form of a mentor and/or from a wider collegial team or community of practice.

Mentors

The origins of the word *mentor* in Greek mythology provide quite an apt analogy for the role of a mentor in the teaching profession. Mentor was the name of Ulysses's friend. He was asked to take care of Telemachus, Ulysses's son, during his father's absence at the Trojan wars. Taking care did not mean simply *looking after* in a passive way but more in the proactive sense of becoming a role model for Telemachus – helping him develop the skills and knowledge he would need in later life. Today, the concept of mentor is used in many professional contexts where it is applied to those who play a particular part in helping others to acquire the abilities and mindsets essential to attain success. While a mentor is a person of experience, this alone is not sufficient to adequately fulfil the role. It embraces that of coach, counsellor and guide and requires, therefore, a capacity to engage with those being mentored in a sympathetic and empathetic manner, so that they will reflect on their work, identify their own strengths and weaknesses, address them appropriately and gradually improve their performance, attitude and results. Pollard stresses some of the skills necessary for the role:

Mentoring is a means of providing support, challenge and extension of the learning of one person through the guidance of another who is more skilled, knowledgeable and experienced, particularly in relation to the context in which learning is taking place.

(Pollard et al, 2008, p 32)

Thus, mentoring involves a structured, sustained partnership between a teacher and their mentee. While it is important that the mentor possesses highly developed personal qualities of empathy and care, it is arguably important that they also have all the characteristics which typify those of the high-status *professional* archetype discussed in Chapter 6. No lesser mentor will suffice.

Learning to teach in a community of practice

Mentoring has always existed in the sense that teachers have always provided advice and support for colleagues, both formally and informally. It is particularly relevant in the context of apprenticeship models of teacher development. Apprenticeship is often seen as an inappropriately limited, work-based learning model for teachers, whereby novice teachers simply seek to replicate the practices of more experienced mentors with a concomitant, formulaic simplification and deficits of critical reflection, innovation and theoretical conceptualisation. Furlong and Maynard (1995) draw on Wenger's (1998) work on situated learning within communities of practice to present an alternative model of apprenticeship in the teaching profession. In such a model, student teachers have a role which combines *peripherality* and *legitimacy* – '*legitimate peripheral participation*' (Wenger, 1998). Wenger suggests that peripherality provides a guided and gradual exposure to full practice so that students/beginning teachers have:

> » lessened intensity, for example, through periods of initial observation followed by reduced teaching loads;
>
> » lessened risk, for example, through close supervision by experienced staff and mentors; or
>
> » lessened production pressures, for example, through less administration and report writing.

Sufficient legitimacy is provided for student teachers to allow them to be treated, in many respects, like other teachers with the support of a well-respected senior teacher as mentor. It is crucially important that they have such legitimacy to '*allow their inevitable stumblings and violations to become opportunities for learning rather than cause for dismissal, neglect or exclusion*' (Wenger, 1998, p 101). In addition, deficits of innovation and intellectual rigour would only exist for the student teachers where they exist for the mentor and if links to higher education institutions are entirely abandoned. If the mentor is the consummate professional (Chapter 6), then an apprenticeship model can bring challenge, criticality and, with the support of local higher education institution staff, may also bring linkages to global educational research and innovation and to appropriate certification/accreditation. There is concern that school-based models of teacher education, which are detached from these revitalising elements, will lead to teachers' roles being rich in localised expertise but lacking the connections to global expertise which can ensure that teachers and their schools do not ossify within the limited geographical imaginations (Chapter 1) and closed horizons of formulaic accountability.

In this context, it is worth noting that Wenger also highlights the importance of schools providing their pupils with a learning place, a locus of engagement, but he cautions that '*there must be more to school learning than learning school*' (1998, p 271). This idea has some resonance with a significant potential drawback of school-based teacher education – for teachers, too, learning within a school must be more than learning that particular school. Wenger suggests that '*students must be able to explore who they are, who they are not and who they could be*' (1998, p 272). The same is true for teachers.

In order to give your trainees the opportunity to start this exploration, the next section populates the quadrant with two proto-professionals from fiction and challenges them to consider the appropriateness of this exemplification and whether it has resonances with themselves as teachers in the twenty-first century.

Proto-professionals from fiction

Extracts from a poem by Anglo-Irish author Oliver Goldsmith and a novel by Charles Dickens present snapshots of two fictional schoolmasters. The anonymous teacher conceived by Goldsmith is unlikely to have completed much of a teacher education journey at all, but he would have been drilled to accumulate extensive amounts of factual knowledge. In respect of perceived status, however, this schoolmaster would rate very highly indeed. Earlier in this poem, Goldsmith described him as a *village statesman*, and in this extract, the schoolmaster is surrounded by awestruck villagers:

> *The village all declared how much he knew;*
> *'Twas certain he could write, and cypher too;*
> *Lands he could measure, terms and tides presage,*
> *And ev'n the story ran that he could gauge.*
> *In arguing too, the parson owned his skill,*
> *For even tho' vanquished, he could argue still;*
> *While words of learned length and thundering sound,*
> *Amazed the gazing rustics ranged around;*
> *And still they gazed, and still the wonder grew,*
> *That one small head could carry all he knew.*
>
> (Oliver Goldsmith, *The Deserted Village*, 1770)

Several decades later and into the next century, Dickens wrote about his schoolmaster:

He and some one hundred and forty other schoolmasters, had been lately turned at the same time, in the same factory, on the same principles, like so many pianoforte legs. He had been put through an immense variety of paces, and had answered volumes of head-breaking questions. Orthography, etymology, syntax and ... geography, and ... land-surveying and levelling, vocal music, and drawing from models, were all at the ends of his ten chilled fingers.

(Charles Dickens, *Hard Times*, 1854)

Mr M'Choakumchild, who has been equipped with an equally immense bank of knowledge, is Dickens's commentary on the earliest graduates of *certificated* teacher training, and although Dickens had erstwhile been a strong advocate of certification for teachers, he presents a somewhat unsympathetic portrait. There are resonances with Hoyle's paradox (Chapter 1) in the ways in which Dickens is scathing about two particular qualities of these teachers.

1. First, their anxiety to obtain professional competence which is portrayed as a rather desperate and shallow learning of vast volumes of facts.

2. Second, Dickens, elsewhere in the novel, is scathing about these newly minted teachers' efforts to ensure a better social status for themselves.

Thus, while Goldsmith's teacher might easily don the role of village statesman, the Mr M'Choakumchilds of this world would not have any choice in the matter. Dickens was very much putting them in their middle-level status place, despite *all they knew* and all that could, of course, be Googled in an instant today.

Today's teachers as craftworkers, technicists and 'deliverologists'

Some 160 years later, developments in teacher education in England might, perhaps, be seen to be enacting a move back in time, of at least a century, featuring both a change of locus and a change of focus in teacher education. The latest developments manifest substantial contrasts with 100 years ago when *'institutional emphasis in initial training was moving in a direction wholly opposite to that of today; that is to say, when the predominant site of training was shifting from school to training institutions'* (Gardiner, 1995, p 191). In addition, more recent developments might be seen to be based on

an understanding of teaching as a) essentially a craft rather than an intellectual activity; b) an apprenticeship model of teacher training that can be located entirely in the workplace; and c) the related assumption that more time spent in schools inevitably – and unproblematically – leads to better and 'more relevant' learning.

(McNamara and Murray, 2013, p 22)

These developments were initiated under the New Labour government (1997–2010) with a greater emphasis on performativity alongside what might be described as a technicist approach to teaching, with teachers uncritically delivering national curricula and prescribed practices (such as the phonetics approach to teaching reading). Richard Pring has described this somewhat restricted professional role for teachers as *'deliverology'* (2012, p 30) in which the teacher's role is only to apply protocols and follow rules, to *deliver* the ideas of others uncritically – for example, synthetic phonics or the seemingly ubiquitous *think, pair and share*. If viewed with a cynic's scrutiny, it is all too readily apparent why a government might seek to cast teachers in such a restricted role. It is also obvious that teachers cannot surrender their professional responsibility to be critical of education policies and initiatives and to adopt new ideas only with a knowledgable and sceptical eye. Giroux articulates the value of an informed and critical professionalism, asserting that

teachers must take responsibility for the knowledge they organise, produce, mediate and translate into practice. If not there is a danger that they come to be seen as simply the technical intervening medium through which knowledge is transmitted to students, erasing themselves in an uncritical reproduction of received wisdom.

(Giroux, 1992, p 120)

The more recent developments in teacher education in England also have their origins in earlier developments in the United States and are driven by the neoliberal agenda of the coalition government – the bywords are *competition* and *choice*. Michael Gove, as Secretary of State for Education, took a very keen interest in models of teacher professionalism. He made it clear that he saw teachers as craftworkers for whom subject knowledge, intuition and local, situational awareness were paramount. The most significant change, however, involved altering the locus of teacher education from universities to schools. This peremptory, large-scale relocation was accompanied and enabled by discourses of derision that positioned those providing university-based teacher education as '*enemies of promise*' (Gove, 2013), as discussed in Chapter 5.

It is, of course, not only Gove who sees teachers as craftworkers. Craftworking is also the model favoured by many teachers – and certainly by many student teachers, too – who seek classroom survival most of all and admire those teachers with secure craft skills, especially in classroom management. In one of the earlier books in this series, Carey Philpott (2014) elaborated on some of the more positive and sophisticated conceptions of teachers as craftworkers. He emphasised '*the integrated nature of knowledge in use and the importance of non-codified forms of knowledge*' in helping student teachers to '*do teaching*' as opposed to, for example, writing essays about it or discussing it online (2014, p 68). Your students might be challenged to read both this chapter and Chapter 8 of Philpott's book and make up their own minds about these important matters in reaction to both the Place Model and their future careers. In doing so, they might consider the following.

» Does craftworking have any place within the teaching profession – should craftworkers be consigned to the lower left quadrant of the Place Model – low-status, precarious professionals?

» Once roles are narrowly defined, technicist and effectively deskilled, might they be replaced by robots? This point is discussed more fully in the next chapter.

» Are technicism, apprenticeship, 'deliverology' and craftworking best viewed as useful parts of what it means to be an effective teacher, but only fragments of a career-long professional learning journey, and, consistent with Hoyle's paradox, unlikely (by themselves) to increase teacher status?

IN A **NUTSHELL**

This chapter has outlined and exemplified some of the most contentious and enduring issues that are raised by this quadrant of the model. Proto-professionalism may be viewed as an early-career transit point for some teachers. Alternatively, for other teachers, it may be a career-long settlement where they will remain because they see this as an uncomplicated and cushy place to become and to be a teacher, or because there is little impetus and/or opportunity to move any further. The admiring gaze of Goldsmith's villagers is harder to attract in the ambient information environment of the early twenty-first century – Hoyle's paradox is alive and well! It is essential that all student teachers (and their mentors) are challenged to contrast this place with the more globally connected, innovative, challenging and complex conceptions of professionalism which are explored in Chapter 6.

Nonetheless, there are plights much worse than being taught by the complacently/ unavoidably incomplete teachers of the proto-professional quadrant. The next chapter moves to the periphery of the Place Model, where the answer to the question *Who is teaching me today?* is *no one* – no teacher is teaching me today.

REFLECTIONS ON **CRITICAL ISSUES**

The unremitting complexity of teaching often comes as a shock to student teachers. A sympathetic mentor can smooth the transition from student to teacher, often by offering the kinds of technicist tips and tricks that can produce the apparently successful early experiences. Over time, these experiences may blend into a comfortable and relatively unchallenging small world of one school or the smaller world of one classroom where one is the local hero, a big fish in a minuscule pond. There they 'can put posters over the glass bit in the door and disappear' (Clarke and Abbott, 2008). This then becomes the miniature and complacent purview of the learner too, unchallenged and unchanged by innovation, critical analysis or ideas from around the world. This quadrant is a constricted place for a teacher and for a profession, not least because it narrows the learner's world too.

Further reading

Chapter 8 in Philpott, C (2014) *Theories of Professional Learning: A Critical Guide for Teacher Educators.* Northwich: Critical Publishing.

Furlong, J and Maynard, T (1995) *Mentoring Student Teachers.* London: Routledge.

CHAPTER 3 | **NO TEACHER**

CRITICAL **ISSUES**

- *Are qualified teachers a necessity, a luxury or an irrelevance?*
- *What challenges might your students face if they were to decide to devote some of their career to teaching in less economically developed parts of the world which have teacher shortages?*
- *In an age of increasingly sophisticated computer applications and the ubiquity of broadband connections to the Internet, is there still a need for local, face-to-face teachers?*
- *Should schooling be compulsory?*

Introduction

This chapter examines a very important part of the model (see page x) which is located outside the axes themselves, where the answer to the question *Who is teaching me today?* is *No one, no teacher is teaching me today.* The chapter begins with a brief consideration of the issues surrounding the relatively recent, policy-sanctioned increase in the numbers of unqualified teachers in England, before focusing on two very contrasting facets of having *no teacher*.

1. The first refers to those pupils who have no teacher available to teach them. The latest UN figures suggest that there are around 57 million primary-school-age learners in this category (UNESCO, 2014).

2. The second (no teacher needed?) considers those learners involved in Sugata Mitra's *The Hole in the Wall Project* (2012) in which learning occurs with a computer, with other learners, but without a teacher. This project is examined alongside the use of eLearning in emergencies such as the Ebola crisis in Africa and, by contrast, the optional recourse to *no teacher* that is the basis of both home schooling and truancy.

No teacher: unqualified teachers

This off-piste part of the Place Model is very relevant to each of the four quadrants, not least because of its intersection with contemporary debates about the employment of unqualified teachers, teacher status and the nature of professional development journeys for teachers. However, it is important to note that, for the purposes of this book, only those who are *qualified* to teach are deemed teachers. The need for teachers to look beyond schools to find answers to the challenges they face, to draw on the robust expertise of others and to build sustainable partnerships is not contested. Teachers need not be the only adults in the classroom, but the employment of unqualified teachers is a contested matter in at least three salient respects. First, there is no globally agreed-upon definition of *a teacher* or, indeed, no delineation of the academic or other qualifications required in order to join the profession. Second, as pointed out in the *Literature Review on Teacher Education in the 21st Century*, which was carried out on behalf of the Scottish Government:

there is little hard evidence to demonstrate the connections between teaching quality, teacher education and pupil outcomes, there is widespread professional agreement that they are positively related.

(Menter et al, 2010, p 45)

Third, in some jurisdictions where teaching qualifications have been mandatory until recently, unqualified teachers are currently permitted to teach, notably in England, where since 2012, academies and free schools have been permitted to employ *teachers* who do not have Qualified Teacher Status. By December 2014, The Shadow Education Secretary, Dr Tristram Hunt, advised that in England:

there were 17,100 unqualified teachers in state-funded schools – a rise of 16% in the past year [and that some] *430,000 children were being taught by unqualified teachers, based on a class size average of 25.3.*

(*The Guardian*, 29 December 2014 [online])

Thus, the number of unqualified staff who are teaching in schools in England is increasing, even while the Department for International Development (DfID, 2013) continues to fund teacher education initiatives in less economically developed countries with the aim of providing qualified teachers for learners in these countries. While this point has a thought-provoking irony, it is also a matter of relative insignificance, given the enormous disparities in the nature of schools and schooling across the globe which mean that millions of learners have no access to qualified teachers.

No teacher: the scale of the problem

Learners with no teacher are the *elephant* in the model. Their plight is often discussed by development agencies but seldom by the profession itself. Tied to the fact that literally no teacher is teaching approximately 57 million primary-school-age children (roughly equivalent to the entire population of England and Scotland) is the equally disconcerting challenge that an additional 1.6 million teachers (almost the same number as the entire population of Northern Ireland) are needed to achieve universal primary education by 2015 (UNESCO, 2012). This date is significant because the second UN Millennium Development Goal set the global aim to

Ensure that, by 2015, children everywhere, boys and girls alike, will be able to complete a full course of primary schooling.

(United Nations, 2000)

There has been considerable success in moving towards this goal, in that the 57 million is only 10 per cent of the potential primary school population and that the number of out-of-school children dropped from 102 million to 57 million from 2000 to 2011 alone (United Nations Statistics Agency, 2013 [online]). Nonetheless, both the law of diminishing returns and predicted future rates of demographic change will continue to challenge any attempts to make further progress. The 2013/4 *Global Monitoring Report* shows that

in Sub Saharan Africa alone there are 30 million children not in school [... and that ...] in 30 years time there will be twice as many African children under the age of 14.

(UNESCO, 2014, p 52)

The impediments to schooling for all learners are well documented and quite thoroughly understood. Poverty, illness, disability, gender, cultural issues, child labour, transportation, migration, disasters and conflict contribute to excluding children from an appropriate education. Nonetheless, the capacity to access schooling cannot be deemed to always have benign impacts either on individuals (as discussed in the next chapter) or on nations:

While increased access to schooling can be shown to help political stability within a country, comparative analysis can question the myth that universal formal education also automatically creates international harmony.

(Davies, 2005, p 357)

No teacher: the impact of gender

A key feature of the problem of access is the gender imbalance in access to, and completion of, schooling. The Worldmapper image of girls not in primary education presents a stark visual of the geography of this problem (Girls not at Primary School; www.worldmapper.org/display.php?selected=201).

The scale of this imbalance and further dimensions of the problem are summed up well by UNESCO:

Girls make up the majority of the world's 61 million out-of-school children. They are less likely than boys to enter primary school. Harmful practices such as early marriage, gender-based violence, discriminatory laws, prevent them from enrolling in or completing school ... women represent two thirds of the world's 775 million illiterates. Despite making breakthroughs in higher education, women still account for just 29 per cent of researchers.

(UNESCO, 2009–2014 [online])

These points were marshalled by UNESCO in the context of their championing of Nobel Peace Prize Laureate Malala Yousafzai, a 15-year-old girl who survived an assassination attempt for her efforts to defend girls' education in Pakistan, after the Taliban outlawed schools for girls in her native Swat Valley. The *I am Malala* tee-shirt campaign mobilised international efforts to end violence against girls who defy local threats to attend school, and the UN Secretary General Ban Ki-moon summed up the reason for the attack: '*By targeting Malala, extremists showed what they feared the most – a girl with a book*' (United Nations, 12 July 2013 [online]). Such incidents are most common in girls' schools, but some of the most horrific attacks have targeted all pupils, as in the incident in December 2014, when 132 children were killed by the Pakistani Taliban in an attack on an army-run school in Peshawar. The link between schooling and violence is discussed further in the next chapter.

In marked contrast to the deficits in female learners noted above, the teaching profession is predominantly female in most parts of the world, particularly in the primary sector, with the exception of Sub-Saharan Africa and South Asia, where women teachers remain the minority (UNESCO, 2012). These are the parts of the world which have the lowest participation rates for girls in education, a fact which sets up ongoing, cyclical challenges, because recruiting female teachers is more difficult when female education and literacy rates are already low. Working in Sub-Saharan Africa, Mulkeen et al suggest that the recruitment of female teachers and principals is 'critical to the expansion and improvement of secondary education systems' (2007, p xi).

Elsewhere, there are concerns about a range of issues related to the feminisation of the profession. Most relevant in this context is the gender-related imbalance in career advancement within the profession, as reported by the Commonwealth Secretariat and UNESCO (2011), across a range of countries. This report quotes Acker's (1989) claim that perceptions of women teachers as non-careerist have impeded teaching's overall claim to professionalisation and that 'loss of status is one of the perceived consequences of teacher feminisation' (Commonwealth Secretariat and UNESCO, 2011, p 16). These assertions have important implications for the position of female/male teachers with respect to both the axes of the Place Model. They are significant in the present context because they may have a detrimental impact on teacher recruitment, making it even more likely that more pupils will have no teacher. This UNESCO report cites a range of quite dated and quite mixed evidence on the matter, suggesting that the issue may be more nuanced and more internationally variable than it might first appear. The Place Model might provide a useful, initial framework for an international comparative study of these complex issues.

A moral imperative for the profession(al)

While there is a teacher shortage in some parts of the world, the European Commission (2013) reported that there were teacher surpluses in some countries, including Portugal and Ireland. This prompts the question as to whether unemployed or underemployed teachers from these countries could help make up the deficit elsewhere. More profoundly, we might consider if teachers everywhere have a moral responsibility to learners who have no teachers. Creating the structures which allow many European-trained teachers to teach in schools in other parts of Europe is a challenging task, but helping those teachers to teach in African schools is a much more complex matter, involving moral, historical, cultural, financial and logistical considerations. While it might be a very beneficial use of a part of the international aid budget – and not an entirely selfless one as with much aid, as the teachers involved could have some very useful CPD – the reality is, of course, much more complicated. Concerns about the perceived or real attitudes of neocolonialism in respect of sending newly qualified teachers to teach in Africa pale into insignificance against the practicalities, because these 57 million out-of-school children are the most difficult to provide with a qualified teacher. The difficulties have little or nothing to do with the pupils themselves. These pupils are often wildly enthusiastic about school. The author vividly remembers asking a pupil who had walked 11 kilometres to get to a Malawian primary school (with 80 pupils per class, no chairs or desks and few books) if she enjoyed school. The girl looked askance and asked, *Who doesn't enjoy school?* So, the problem is not with the pupils but the fact that these 57 million children are the ones who live either in remote areas with poor roads, no electricity and little potable water or in the world's most disaster- or conflict-ridden environments.

These learners are going to be difficult to reach and to teach, although, in relative terms, not so difficult at all. The World Bank (no date) estimates a cost of between 10 and 30 billion US dollars (it is very difficult to be more accurate) to meet the second Millennium Development Goal. In a world where military expenditure in 2013 totalled $1747 billion according to the Stockholm International Peace Research Institute (SIPIRI, 2015), perhaps this is most of all a failure of will, but also a failure of compassion in an increasingly unequal world.

Reaching and teaching learners using technology: in emergencies

In some countries, the intervention of particular crises can cause the closure of existing schools, and increasingly organisations such as UNICEF and UNHCR are seeking research evidence around the best ways to support education during and after conflict/disasters (Smith, 2005). The 2014–15 Ebola crises in West Africa have led the Ministry of Education, Science and Technology in Sierra Leone and UNICEF (2014) to make use of the ubiquity of mobile phones even in the most remote areas to allow isolated learners to have at least some access to lessons. In late 2014, the Ebola crisis left 1.7 million pupils unable to attend schools or even to meet with their friends. Courses have been developed by teachers in English, mathematics, social studies, physical and health education, psychosocial and life skills, hygiene and hand-washing, and these are broadcast to pupils in their homes through a network of 41 radio stations across the country. This basic form of eLearning has met with problems around regular electricity supply for phone charging and is, of necessity, based on a very one-sided, solitary and didactic pedagogy.

There are, however, some academics who suggest that teachers are not necessary for children's education, most notably Sugata Mitra and his assertions based around the early stages of *The Hole in the Wall Project* in some of the poorest and most remote parts of the globe.

Reaching and teaching learners using technology: no teacher needed?

Arguably *The Hole in the Wall Project* is most famous, or perhaps infamous, for its creator's repeated assertions that *no teacher is needed*. This, of course, is only part of the story, a part which seems to be diminishing as the project develops. It began with a computer which was embedded in the wall of a kiosk within a slum area in Kalkaji, New Delhi,

India. The computer had a touch pad and used a Windows-based operating system (in English). A video camera was positioned nearby to record the use of the device. Mitra (2012) described how the local children who came to explore the kiosk computer had little formal education or knowledge of either English or computers, but within eight months they claimed to have '*taught themselves*' how to use the touch pad, access the programmes and use the Internet. Mitra described the children's learning as '*minimally invasive education*' and suggested that it '*uses the learning environment to generate an adequate level of motivation to induce learning in groups of children, with minimal, or no, intervention by a teacher*' (Mitra et al, 2005, p 2).

These kiosk experiments have been trialled in several countries, and the project has moved on to the so-called *granny cloud* and Self-Organised Learning Environments (SOLEs), which are based within schools in the UK, with some retired teachers (hence, *grannies*) providing support to the children. The focus here is on allowing learners independently to seek answers to *big questions* which are derived from the local curriculum. As a geography teacher educator, the author found the sample geography question – '*Where is Botswana and what is it famous for?*' (Mitra, 2012) – to be not remotely typical of school-level geography in the early twenty-first century, at least in the UK. Nonetheless, Mitra describes the changing role of the teacher in SOLEs as follows:

The teacher's role becomes bigger and stranger than ever before: She must ask her 'learners' about things she does not know herself. Then she can stand back and watch as learning emerges.

(Mitra, 2012, n.p.)

Your student teachers might wish to make up their own minds about *The Hole in the Wall Project*. As a starting point, they might watch Sugata Mitra and David Leat discuss the latest developments in the project at the 2014 BERA conference (www.youtube.com/watch?v=sNk47txPVUY; see also Mitra, 2012). *The Hole in the Wall Project* is no longer based around *no teacher*. In fact, it has come to resemble more conventional social constructivist learning supported by schools and technology. Perhaps this is inevitable as the project develops and faces

significant challenges of negotiating the relationships with the school, the teacher as a mediator, and the kinds of content, instruction and curriculum that it can allow to seep into these relatively free spaces without compromising on the underlying tenets of innovative pedagogy.

(Arola, 2005, p 700)

Questions have been raised about the lack of independent empirical evidence on project outcomes (Arora, 2005). In addition, it has been suggested that Mitra is advocating an anti-teacher neoliberalism, as is stridently argued and debated, for example, on the eltjam blog (www.eltjam.com/why-we-should-be-afraid-of-the-big-bad-wolf-sugata-mitra-and-the-neoliberal-takeover-in-sheeps-clothing/). Further, it might be argued that Mitra would not have been permitted to set up the computers without firewalls in some more economically developed countries and that the project (in which data logs show that pornography was accessed on some machines) was built on taking advantage of the more lenient child protection laws in India. Certainly, it seems that the successive project developments are beginning to resemble conventional formal schooling, albeit within a social constructivist paradigm.

By contrast, Bill Gates's (1995) predictions on the future of eLearning in his book *The Road Ahead* pointed to the value of learners everywhere having online access to the world's best teachers. The advent of open schooling (operating in British Colombia, Canada, since 1919) and, much more recently, of Massive, Open, Online Courses (MOOCs) has brought free access to courses *taught* (at least, in part, *delivered*) by eminent teachers, although these are often unaccredited, short-term ventures which are mere tasters for courses with fees which are well beyond the reach of those in the poorest areas of the world.

Some high-quality, school-level online tutorials such as those of the Khan Academy (www.khanacademy.org) for mathematics and physics (subjects with their own distinctive, international languages) remain free to access, as do some educational apps, although the latter may only be accessed via expensive tablet devices linked to the Internet and often deploy a limited range of pedagogies with a particular emphasis on drill and practice. Seamus Heaney, speaking on his 86th birthday, described the use of the Internet to find out things as '*a sort of technological one night stand*' (2012). Heaney would, I suppose, have found support for this view in more sophisticated eLearning such as the study reported by Bayne (2015) in the introduction of *Teacherbot*, the automated teacher presence for the course Twitter feed, developed by a team at the University of Edinburgh for the MOOC which had around 90,000 students. Algorithms were used to control the Teacherbot's responses to students' tweets, and there is evidence of interactive dialogue between students and *Botty* (their affectionate nickname for Teacherbot) around curricular (eg, providing students with relevant citations), organisational (eg, assignment submission dates) and more light-hearted elements (eg, about whether Botty was having a weekend off).

On the other hand, while the seminal Oxford Martin School study of how susceptible a range of 702 jobs are to computerisation (Frey and Osborne, 2013) showed that about 47 per cent of US employment is at risk, teaching was among those occupations least likely to be at risk. In addition, the study evidenced strong negative relationships between an occupation's probability of computerisation and both wages and educational attainment. It is worth noting that if wages are taken to be a proxy for status and educational attainment as a proxy for career-long professional learning (even while recognising that these are limited and partial proxies), the study does support the key propositions of the Place Model.

Nonetheless, we are a long way from replacing a teacher with a machine ... even as I type this sentence, I can hear my unborn grandchildren laughing at my naiveté, but I am inclined to agree with Arthur C. Clarke (1980, p 96) who asserted that '*any teacher that can be replaced by a robot, should be*'.

No teacher needed? Home education

In the UK, as in many other counties, education is compulsory, but attending school is not. Thus, a child may be educated at home rather than in school. Those providing home education (often a child's parents/guardians) do not have to be qualified to do so, nor are they required to follow a formal curriculum. However, there are periodic attempts to regulate and evaluate home schooling and to ascertain the learners' perspectives on the matter. The OECD (2010) reported that, among its 30 member states, in the Czech Republic (at lower secondary level), Germany, Japan, Mexico, South Korea, the Slovak Republic and Spain, home schooling is not a legal means to provide compulsory education. The matter hit global headlines when a German pupil sought political asylum in the US on the basis that home education is not permitted in Germany (ABC News, 2013 [online]). Accurate figures for the numbers of children whose parents/guardians opt to teach children at home are difficult to ascertain, but the total figures are relatively small – for example, the National Center for Education Statistics (NCES, 2013 [online]) reported that approximately 3 per cent of the US school-age population were home-schooled during the 2011–12 school year. Questions have been raised about the content, value base and teaching quality of home schooling, and attempts to introduce inspections are frequently resisted (Kunzman and Gaither, 2013).

No teacher wanted? Truancy

Pupils may also choose to absent themselves from school, and many do. A recent OECD survey showed considerable variation across the globe and also demonstrated (unsurprisingly) a negative relationship between high levels of truancy and high exam grades. The reasons are many and varied, and only some have causal links to teachers – for example, a study examining the impacts of truancy in relation to the PISA tests suggest that truancy is associated with poorer student performance in mathematics (OECD PISA, 2014, p 1 [online]).

An insatiable demand for quality

While Moon and Umar suggest that 'globally there is almost an insatiable demand for teachers' (Moon, 2013, p 227), considerable progress has been made, even in the very poorest parts of the world, in reducing the number of pupils who have no access to qualified teachers, despite sharply rising demand for secondary teachers (Mulkeen et al, 2007). Mitra has developed a novel, but not entirely unproblematic, approach to allowing such pupils to use technology to support their own learning independently. Questions as to whether teachers can or should be replaced by computers or robots seem likely to persist. In many countries, schooling at the hands of qualified teachers is considered an unquestionable advantage for all and is compulsory where available – and where not available, is often a key development priority. In some countries where schooling is available, and often where it is free of charge, truancy is an ongoing concern and home-schooled pupils form a small minority whose experience of education is often underevaluated and underresearched.

In some parts of the world, there are, however, learners whose fates might be deemed much worse than having no possibility of access to a teacher to teach them today, whether by parental choice or by unfortunate necessity. The next chapter moves back within the axes of the Place Model, to the quadrant occupied by the precarious professionals. From that vantage point, it is easy to see why the post-2015 goals for education target evaluating and improving the quality of education, with a particular focus on the quality of teachers.

IN A **NUTSHELL**

Approximately 57 million learners in the very poorest parts of the world have no teachers to teach them, though no choice of their own, and attempts to alleviate this problem face significant challenges. On the other hand, there are those who suggest that qualified teachers are not necessary even though there is little agreement as to what qualifications should be required in order to teach. *The Hole in the Wall Project*, radio-based learning in emergency situations, and home schooling provide contrasting environments for learning in the absence of a teacher and challenge us to consider if qualified teachers are a necessity, a luxury or an irrelevance.

REFLECTIONS ON **CRITICAL ISSUES**

This chapter addresses some thorny and important issues that relate to learners having no teacher by choice or by misfortune – some would say, by good fortune. The inequities in teacher provision and disparities in requirements for teachers to be qualified mean that there is very considerable variation in provision, uptake and qualifications of teachers. The profession must be able to define and defend teacher education qualifications and would then be on firmer ground from which to eloquently, assiduously and robustly demand that qualified teachers teach all learners. In addition, they should recognise that other adults have a range of roles to play in enriching education and actively seek ways to address both teacher shortages and pupil truancy.

Further reading

Arora, P (2005) Hope-in-the-Wall? A Digital Promise for Free Learning. *British Journal of Educational Technology*, 41(5): 689–702.

European Commission (2013) *Study on Policy Measures to Improve the Attractiveness of the Teaching Profession in Europe: Final report*. [online] Available at: www.ec.europa.eu/education/library/study/2013/teaching-profession1_en.pdf (accessed 9 September 2015).

The Net Mums website outlines the pros and cons of home education: www.netmums.com/children/home-education (accessed 9 September 2015) and a focused bibliography on home-schooling in the UK has been created by Ruth Morton: www.homeeducation.wordpress.com/bibliography/ (accessed 9 September 2015).

CHAPTER 4 | THE PRECARIOUS PROFESSIONALS

CRITICAL **ISSUES**

- Is it better to have no teacher at all than the damaging, unprofessional teachers of this chapter?
- What can be done to ensure that teachers behave professionally? Is it ever right to behave unprofessionally?
- Why/how/by whom might you be struck off as a teacher?
- What can the teaching profession do to retain its best teachers?
- What are the key values of the teaching profession?

Introduction

This chapter considers the quadrant (see page x) in which teachers have low status and also have not progressed their professional development beyond a very basic initial qualification. Two worrying categories of teachers are discussed in this chapter: those who might be described as *unprofessional*, and those who are unlikely to remain in the profession – the *transitory* teachers. In both cases, their position in the teaching profession might be described as precarious.

While much attention has been paid to the 2013/14 UNESCO *Global Monitoring Report* declaration that 57 million learners were not in school (as discussed in Chapter 2), the report also contained a statistic which is, in some ways, much more disturbing: '*at least 250 million children cannot read or count, even if they have spent 4 years in school*'. Concerns about literacy and numeracy, in particular, have meant that the post-Millennium Development Goals agenda is very much centred on the quality of education and, integral to this, on the quality of teachers. The reality of schooling for many learners challenges the assumption (often backed by policy and coercion) that mass public schooling is an unquestionably good thing, with the corollary that all teachers always act in the best interests of all learners.

While Chapter 6 seeks to delimit the characteristics of a professional teacher, the current chapter begins by confronting those teachers who might be described as the antithesis of these exemplary professionals – the unprofessionals. The chapter examines the characteristics of such teachers and the main reasons why they exist and persist. In addition, some *legitimate* and some subversive reasons for unprofessional behaviour are considered. Before your students become teachers, they need to be aware of why, how and by whom they might come to be removed from the profession. The chapter will also discuss the reduced professional trajectories of those low-status, poorly educated teachers who are all too common in some less economically developed countries. Teacher retention is a salient problem in such countries, where teachers are often badly paid, inadequately supported and held in such low esteem that many feel forced to consider other career options. The chapter concludes with a brief examination of some potential solutions to the problems presented by unprofessional teachers and transitory teachers.

Unprofessional teachers

The characteristics of unprofessional teachers

Referring to their work in African schools, Lynne Davies and colleagues itemised the characteristics of unprofessional teachers as follows:

- » *absenteeism;*
- » *unplanned lessons;*
- » *the double-jobber;*
- » *instances of sexual abuse;*
- » *strong use of corporal punishment …*
- » *hostility to and distance from children.*

(2005, pp 35–39)

Reflecting on their pre-service experiences, some such characteristics were echoed in a recent study of student teacher mentoring by the author and colleagues from African universities, when student teachers from Malawi were interviewed about the nature and extent of the support they received while on teaching practice (Clarke et al, 2013). The data suggested both alarming quality issues and wilful unprofessionalism in a country where, although there are many excellent teachers, most are poorly paid and poorly esteemed, and too many of them live down to low expectations. The following are extracts from a student teacher focus group discussing the unsatisfactory support they received in schools:

- » *I did not get the help I expected – the English teacher had quit, so I had extra classes and was the only teacher. I'm now discovering mistakes … now that I've asked other teachers in other subjects …*

- » *Teachers teach in more than one school to make more money. The school that I was in has more than 100 pupils in a class and the teachers just handed over and went away.*

- » *Teachers do not have time and off-load some of their work, but have no time for you.*

- » *Teachers are money makers … they are off doing other things.*

(Clarke et al, 2013)

Moon and Umar (2013) pointed towards the longer term impacts of such persistent problems on learners, quoting Buckler's (2012) in-depth study of the lives of teachers in a number of countries in Sub-Saharan Africa. This study presented a profession where standards were worryingly inconsistent, varying from the excellent to the atrocious.

We have educators whose accomplishments exceed even the high expectations placed on them by the system and the community. They are the heroes of our schooling system and there are many of them ... Sadly we have a minority of educators who not only fail to give their best in the classroom, but contravene school rules by, for instance, arriving late at work in the morning, and engaging in criminal acts and sexual abuse. The harm that such behaviour inflicts on our schooling system, on the reputation of the teaching fraternity, and on the next generation of South Africans is very high.

(Buckler, 2012, cited in Moon and Umar, 2013, p 237).

Such models of extreme unprofessionalism may have grave physical and psychological effects on individual pupils. They also have consequences for the nature of learning that is possible in schools. The work of Freire and Giroux and others on critical pedagogy laid key foundations for the revised curricula of the early twenty-first century (including that in Malawi; for example, MoEST, 2000) which promote active learning strategies within democratic classrooms. Such pedagogies are clearly at odds with the unprofessionalism that is intimated above.

Of course, such unprofessionalism may still be found among teachers in more economically developed countries. However, while there is all too abundant evidence of historical cases of child abuse in educational settings, in the early twenty-first century their infrequency is such that individual cases are likely to hit the headlines and attract the urgent attention of both the police and professional bodies (as discussed below). Just as unprofessional behaviour is not confined to less economically developed countries, neither is it constrained by the child protection legislation of many economically developed countries or by national borders, as evidenced in the recent case of Bill Vahey, a teacher in an elite, private, international school in London where the chairperson of the board of governors was the former Chief Inspector of Schools in England and Wales. It is suspected that Vahey drugged, molested and photographed many pupils during school trips. In addition, it has transpired that he had a previous conviction for child molestation in California, that the London school had failed to seek references and that there were deficiencies in the school's child protection procedures (*The Independent*, 2014). Parents/guardians of current and former pupils from the London school faced the dilemma of whether they wished to find out if their children were molested by Vahey. Harber's (2004) book, *Schooling as Violence,* provides an extensive international analysis and should be on the reading list of all teacher education courses, not least as an antidote to those who unquestioningly assume the benevolence of schooling. The chapter on sexual violence (much of it committed by teachers) is not for the fainthearted.

While such behaviour seems to be a diminishing phenomenon, teacher malpractice around public examinations seems to be an increasingly common form of unprofessionalism. Publication of examination results in comparative school league tables and an increasing emphasis on data analysis during school inspections have tempted teachers to engage in various forms of cheating, such as helping pupils with coursework or altering their answers. In the UK, this has led to the introduction of more *tightly controlled assessment* at General

Certificate in Secondary Education (GCSE) level, replacing less stringently monitored coursework, but there is evidence that there has been dishonesty in controlled assessment too. In 2014, the regulatory body, OFQUAL (Office of Qualifications and Examinations Regulation), reported a substantial increase in penalties issued to both individual staff and to schools and colleges in respect of irregularities in practice around examinations:

There were 217 penalties issued to schools and colleges. This is up from 140 last year. Seventy-two per cent of these penalties were written warnings.

(OFQUAL, 2014)

In Atlanta, Georgia, nine school teachers, principals and administrators who were convicted of participating in a widespread conspiracy to inflate students' scores on state tests were given prison sentences (*Washington Post*, no date). This case has prompted comparisons with corrupt Wall Street bankers and has called into question the negative impact of using test scores for performance management. In the US, new legislation is planned to ratchet up this process so that teacher education providers will also be judged and compared on the basis of the test scores of the pupils of their former student teachers.

Reasons for unprofessionalism

While some teachers may reluctantly, but defiantly, seek to justify the cases of examination malpractice exemplified above, the reasons for unprofessionalism are generally more complex and may vary substantially between individual cases. However, where abuse is widespread, the reasons are often worryingly systemic. Clive Harber and colleagues have drawn on extensive work across Africa to identify the following as the reasons for such behaviour: '*occupation hampered by poor training, lack of resources, low or unpaid salaries and low levels of continuing professional development*' (Harber and Davies, 1997, cited in Harber, 2012, p 60; Harber and Stephens, 2009). Much of this speaks to the relationship between teacher status and career-long professional learning which is at the heart of the Place Model.

A further long-standing and fundamentally systemic reason why teachers who exhibit the characteristics associated with this kind of unprofessionalism can continue to remain in schools (and also why they matter so much) is because of the widely recognised imbalance of power in the classroom, which is well portrayed in Ginnott's reflections on his own practice:

I have come to a frightening conclusion: I am the decisive element in the classroom. It is my personal approach that creates the climate. It is my daily mood that makes the weather. As a teacher I possess tremendous power to make a child's life miserable or joyless. I can be a tool of torture or an instrument of inspiration. I can humiliate, humor, hurt or heal. In all situations, it is my response that decides whether a crisis will be escalated or de-escalated, and a child humanized or dehumanized.

(Ginott, 1972, pp 15–16)

Such candid admissions touch on the fact that teachers have agency and responsibility around their own professionalism and that of their colleagues. The exercise of this agency can lead to them choosing to break/subvert the rules or to *whistleblowing*, as is discussed towards the end of the chapter where ways to deal with unprofessionalism are considered.

Transitory teachers

A second type of precarious professional consists of those whose tenure in the teaching profession is unlikely to last long because of a range of factors, including low-status, fragile conditions of service including salary, accommodation and safety, and also limited capacity to advance their careers. These issues have their most extreme manifestations in the world's poorest countries. Moon and Umar sum up the key problems around teacher retention in less economically developed countries, noting, too, some interesting complexities around the connections between status and CPD:

In countries growing at the rates of Brazil, China, India and sub-Saharan Africa new structures of employment are appearing. The sort of person who became a teacher is now lured away to other knowledge-based professions. Those who become teachers are subject to similar temptations. The teacher retention rates in many school systems hover around 50 percent or thereabouts after five years. Many qualification upgrading courses, rather than contributing to the improvement of the school system, function as a bridge to higher paid jobs, with improved status, outside education.

(Moon and Umar, 2013, p 237)

Of course, these issues are also found in the most developed countries, particularly during periods of strong economic growth, although there is also considerable variability both within and between countries, and teacher shortages are often greatest in science subjects.

The impacts of rapid staff turnover are well documented. A large-scale study (850,000 fourth- and fifth-grade students aged over 8 years) in the public school system in New York City reported that

students in grade levels with higher turnover score lower in both English language arts (ELA) and math and that these effects are particularly strong in schools with more low-performing and Black students. Moreover, the results suggest that there is a disruptive effect of turnover beyond changing the distribution in teacher quality.

(Ronfelt et al, 2013, p 4)

The following sections consider some salient solutions to the problems of transitory and unprofessional teachers.

What can be done about the unprofessionals?

This section starts by discussing teachers who feel compelled to break the rules or to *blow the whistle* and then examines the role of professional bodies in dealing with unprofessional teachers.

Teachers may feel compelled to *break the rules*, to ignore, subvert, challenge or contravene policy. Your students might like to consider the following example which was widely known and reported but, until recently, largely ignored by the authorities within Northern Ireland. Although 11+ transfer tests (at the end of primary education) were abolished in 2008, they were replaced by illegal tests used by local grammar schools to select their pupils on the basis of academic performance. In early 2015, the Department of Education wrote to 11 primary schools to express concerns at the possible coaching of pupils for the unregulated tests during core teaching hours (BBC News, 2015). Reports of this activity came from parents and also from teachers who were under parental pressure to coach the pupils outside school hours, but also during core teaching times. The abolition of the 11+ transfer test has been very controversial with several local political parties supporting it and others (including Sinn Fein, the party of the Minister of Education) against the test. Teachers can find themselves within a political maelstrom with additional pressures coming from parents, from pupils and from school principals. It is as yet unclear how some teachers brought these particular matters to the attention of the relevant government department, but in the UK a charity, Public Concern at Work (PCAW), reported a jump of 44 per cent of cases of whistleblowing in education between early 2011 and early 2012 (www.pcaw. org.uk). Your student teachers should be made aware that whistleblowing can be a very daunting and unrewarding process and they should be given an opportunity to discuss the issue. PCAW provides training materials and advice for both teachers and employers. Students should also learn about their local professional body for teaching (where one exists).

Professional bodies in some countries have created codes of ethics and have, in some cases, the power to remove teachers from professional registers – ie, to prevent them from teaching in schools. The General Teaching Council for Scotland (GTCS) was set up in 1965 and, since becoming independent from government in 2012, is *'the world's first independent, self-regulating, professional body for teaching'*. It maintains the register of teachers in Scotland and has developed a *Code of Professionalism and Conduct* (GTCS, 2012). In addition, it has the power to investigate and adjudicate on the Fitness to Teach of registrants. Your students might usefully be encouraged to find out about some cases in which teachers have been removed (*struck off*) from the register and about how teacher registration and conduct are governed in their jurisdiction. They might consider who should have the authority to end a teacher's career. The General Teaching Council for Northern Ireland (GTCNI) does not yet have full independence from government, nor does it have the capacity to remove teachers from its register – senior civil servants do this. It has, however, developed a specific list of professional values which your students might consider:

» *trust*

» *honesty*

» *commitment*

» *respect*

» *fairness*

» *equality*

» *integrity*

» *tolerance*

» *service*

(GTCNI, 2007, p 2)

The students might be asked to rank these values, to add to them (should they believe this to be appropriate) and to decide if they think that any are superfluous. The author's student teachers often remove tolerance (considered unnecessary as it is deemed a less demanding component of *respect*) while adding *optimism*. Your students might be invited to consider whether what should be added – in order to include recognition of the persistent realities of unprofessionalism and of both the academic and the practical dimensions of teaching – is not optimism alone but the phrase widely attributed to Antonio Gramsci, '*pessimism of the intellect and optimism of the will*'.

What can be done about the transitory teachers?

It can be hard for students in more economically developed countries to imagine the working conditions of teachers in rural schools in the Global South. Maslow's Hierarchy of Needs (1943) identifies the basic human needs (shelter, food, security, self-actualisation) which must be met before there can be sufficient motivation to improve and maintain the quality of education. In these areas, it is meeting those very basic needs which is the key to teacher retention.

Kadzamira (2006) and Kayuni and Tambulasi (2007) provide candid country overviews of teachers and teacher education for Malawi, both of which point to absenteeism, double jobbing and poor retention. Interestingly, in relation to this sector of the Place Model, Kadzamira cites two main reasons for this – low esteem, which is reflected in poor conditions of service, and few opportunities for CPD. In respect of the latter, Kadzamira unequivocally notes that a lack of scope *for training and seminars* (for teachers, relative to other professions where these are more common) is viewed as problematic because these events also afford opportunities for receiving additional financial allowances. The author has often heard this factor mentioned in conversation, but it is not admitted officially. However, it does provide a striking insight into the realities of life for some teachers in the poorest parts of the world and the relatively simple measures that are required to lay foundations for good retention rates. Once these needs are met, career-long professional learning opportunities are prerequisites for both retention and quality.

In more economically developed countries, it is argued that the revolving door via which new entrants quickly become recent leavers can be removed through the consistent implementation of a diverse (and expensive) range of proactive measures. In Britain, Barmby (2006) highlights the importance of workload and pupil behaviour, pointing out that policymakers need to recognise that supportive induction is essential. A large-scale meta-analysis (Ingersoll and Strong, 2011) in the US found conflicting evidence on the impact of induction and mentorship on teacher retention. Smethem (2007) earlier emphasised the importance of professional satisfaction as part of the moral purpose of teaching, suggesting that the marketisation of education and intensification of teachers' work may contribute to teacher shortages.

Teacher retention seems set to become a bigger problem, over longer timescales, in many more economically developed countries, as the retirement age for teachers is increased over the coming years. This is one of the issues discussed in the next chapter, which examines the *de-professionalised* quadrant of the Place Model.

IN A **NUTSHELL**

The precarious professionals cause damage to the profession itself, to learners and to wider society. Teacher retention is essential in order to ensure that pupils at least have an opportunity to be taught. It is an unusual problem in that it is one that seems to afflict both the very poorest countries and also those experiencing the highest levels of wealth and the strongest economic growth. The unprofessionals of this quadrant are widely pervasive but might be viewed as the remnants of a primordial quagmire from which the profession has, to a varying extent, escaped over the years. Taken together, the unprofessional and transitory teachers of this quadrant of the Place Model are a pernicious bane on schooling. Arguably, though, it is the latter who can have the most appalling impacts. The most malevolently unprofessional teachers leave a trail of battered, abused, disillusioned, illiterate and innumerate pupils in their wake, and this damage may have longer term, intergenerational repercussions for the learners and their descendants.

At the same time, there are those teachers who have completed long, complex and, perhaps, even illustrious professional journeys, but who might be described as *de-professionalised*. They are the focus of the next chapter.

REFLECTIONS ON **CRITICAL ISSUES**

All professions have unprofessional members and many, too, have problems in retaining staff, especially where jobs are poorly esteemed and rewarded and where training is inadequate. Such precarious teachers can and do wreak havoc in schools, especially in the very poorest parts of the world where, arguably, learners are in most need of the very best teachers. The role of professional bodies in defining and policing standards cannot be overestimated, and the wider role of these bodies in ensuring the status of the whole profession is likewise an invaluable asset for teachers and learners alike.

Further reading

Harber, C (2004) *Schooling as Violence: How Schools Damage Pupils and Societies.* Abingdon: Routledge.

Smethem, L (2007) Retention and Intention in Teaching Careers: Will the New Generation Stay? *Teachers and Teaching: Theory and Practice*, 13(5): 465–80.

CRITICAL **ISSUES**

• *How might a student teacher best defend themselves from staffroom cynics?*

• *Do we need educational dragons to robustly and positively represent the best interests of the profession, of learners?*

• *Who are your local educational dragons?*

Introduction

In this quadrant (see page x) are placed teachers who have considerable expertise, having made a long professional learning journey but who, nonetheless, might be placed in a position of low status in the model. Such a situation is exemplified in this chapter by teachers of two contrasting types:

1. those who have (to a greater or lesser extent) chosen to join the perennial ranks of the staffroom cynics; and

2. those cast into this position as the objects of '*discourses of derision*', deployed by those who seek to create the '*rhetorical space in which to articulate reform*' (Ball, 2008, p 104).

While members of the first group might be seen, at their worst, to have chosen to reposition themselves, those belonging to the second group may be seen to have been consigned to this putative position in the Place Model based on politicised castigation within the media.

These two groups of teachers are, indeed, strange bedfellows, but, as the chapter will show, both groups share the potential to be conspicuous, significant and even ferocious actors within ongoing education debates. This quadrant should, it is argued, bear the warning used by medieval mapmakers for dangerous or uncharted areas, *Beware, here be dragons!* Typically the staffroom cynics (the deriders) respond to their self-banishment with an artillery barrage, often coated in either apparent sincerity or blatant sarcasm, warning student teachers not to join the profession or encouraging subversion of professional practice and policy. By contrast, senior teacher educators (the derided), in both the US (from the late 1990s) and England (about 10 years later), have responded to political derision by becoming, perhaps belatedly, strident champions for the profession, or at least for their view of the profession, one which has its roots in university-based teacher education.

Understandably, it is the staffroom cynics who are of most immediate interest to student teachers who fall into the gap '*between the chalkface and the ivory towers*' (Murray, 2002) and who may never get to meet some of the most eminent teacher professionals. However, students should not be unaware of the great teacher education debates of the early twenty-first century. The Place Model permits some access to the heart of these debates by *populating* this quadrant with some of the senior educational actors within the ideological maelstrom which seems set to shape the profession across the globe for many years to come. First, however, it is important to examine the more commonplace roles and realities of the staffroom cynics.

Staffroom cynics (the deriders)

They stay young, they stay young and they stay young, and you get older and older and older, it's the same old pattern. That's what I dislike about being a teacher.

This is a quote from one of the participants in Sikes's (1985, p 27) seminal work on the *life cycle of the teacher*, which used the life history method to examine the careers of a sample of art teachers and science teachers, aged between 25 and 70 years. Some teachers in *Phase 5* of the life cycle (*50–55-plus age range*) reported being perceived as '*past it*' by both colleagues and pupils and that '*retirement becomes an increasingly attractive prospect*' (Sikes, 1985, p 54).

Some of these teachers may have once been very enthusiastic and/or been highly accomplished teachers who have made long and complex learning journeys but have given up for some reason. Others may be long-term, serial cynics who have managed to remain in the profession and may leave generations of damaged learners and student teachers in their wake. This is a problem which seems destined to grow as a result of increases in the length of the working life of teachers in most countries. In England and Wales, the Teachers Working Longer Review Group is examining '*the health and deployment implications of teachers working longer as a result of the normal pension-age increase*' (to 67 years). Maintaining professional vigour seems destined to be a particular challenge in teaching where the '*aging of members is likely to assume increasing significance for the cultures, ethos and outcomes of schools*' (Sikes, 1985, p 27).

Student teachers are all too often confronted with salvos of toxic cynicism from teachers who have become disillusioned by the profession and want, or say they want, to save their young colleagues from *the mistake they made* in joining the profession in the first place. Alternatively, they may feel that they have missed out on important promotions, may be seeking to wield power without responsibility or may simply be cynical about particular aspects of school policy. It would be easy for students to become discouraged while listening to such barrages, especially if a student is already finding teaching difficult. Lucas noted extracts from student teacher responses to a questionnaire distributed within Sheffield University Division of Education in the summer term, 1985. Your trainees might be asked if these have any resonance in the early twenty-first century:

I have had so few encouraging comments that I can't actually remember any examples.

... some teachers seem to have such a jaundiced view of the profession, I wonder why they remain teachers!

(School) was pretty demoralising ... we had a weekly meeting with the person in charge of students who was desperate to move away from the school. He kept stressing what a horrible, underpaid job it is – and how much harder it has become since pupils have become 'less controllable' ...

Get out while you can ...

Some quite bitter comments in response to me complaining of exhaustion – 'Just wait till you do it full-time; all I've done this term is work and sleep'. 'You have to get used to it. It doesn't get any better, you just keep going because you can't afford to give up'. 'All your [sic] doing now is teaching, wait 'till you've got all the paper work and the bloody meetings'.

And a lot of depression about control problems – 'You get so much abuse, it gets to you after a while'. 'None of them want to be here; I've given up thinking I can teach them anything; they don't want to know'.

During my first TP there were a few teachers in the Staffroom who expressed cynicism and discouragement. They were critical of conscientious teachers and advised me to 'do as little as possible' – 'no-one thinks any more of you for doing extra, they will just take advantage of you' – 'You'll learn!' These were not members of the Humanities Dept who offered support, advice and encouragement throughout the practice and offered positive examples of commitment and conscientious professionalism.

My second teaching practice experience reflects the growing disillusionment among teachers over professional status and pay and the employment situation. Many more teachers expressed dissatisfaction and open discouragement.

(Lucas, 1988, p 95)

Preparing student teachers to deal with these cynics, inoculating them against such scepticism, while ensuring they have a mind that is open enough to perceive some truths amidst the tirades, is a vitally important part of teacher education. Student teachers should be given the chance to undertake a role play that includes a typical onslaught. In this way, they could build a repertoire of defences which might include:

» considering if there is any corroborated truth in the words of the derider;

» avoiding their company; and

» actively seeking the support of the teacher tutor and the advice and company of more positive colleagues.

Taking firm charge of a professional learning trajectory and seeking to build one's own professional agency are the best proactive responses. Student teachers might be helped by the accumulated wisdom of a second set of occupants in this quadrant, the derided, although it seems unlikely that their paths will cross.

The derided

An initial reading of Professor Richard Pring's recent book, *The Life and Death of Secondary Education for All* (2012), may surprise the reader, in that Pring laments the demise of Her Majesty's Inspectorate of Schools (HMI). However, he is only lamenting the demise of one particular role played by the HMI:

Until the 1970s Her Majesty's Inspectorate, HMI, was fiercely independent of politicians and government. No minister, not even the prime minister, would dare to speak about education without the script being approved by the Chief Inspector HMI … their carefully gathered evidence from around the country (the 'ears and eyes' of the minister), protected the independence of the profession.

(Pring, 2012, p 120)

Pring is suggesting that the HMI would not ever have been publically treated with derision in the way that senior teacher educators (including himself) have been and that this disparagement is both a reflection and a consequence of diminishing teacher status. The absence of a powerful HMI has given government ministers in England more leeway to force though large-scale changes in the educational landscape virtually unchallenged, except latterly by the *dragons*.

Student teachers will have little time to explore the political and ideological underpinnings of these arguments, but should be aware that teacher education and professional development constitute a contested landscape. They should be given the opportunity to consider alternative viewpoints and to decide where they stand on these important issues. If they become teachers who are not capable of taking a resolute and reasonable stand on these matters, they may find it difficult to assert professional agency and, without this, may find it increasingly difficult to claim that they are professionals at all. Even if they choose not to join the debate, they should, at least, be able to critique the key arguments, their origins and their future trajectories within the game plans of governments of different political hues. In particular, they should be made aware of the huge tectonic shifts in relation to teacher education and professionalism in the US and in England and of the contrasting professionalisation approaches being perused in Finland, Scotland, Ireland and elsewhere.

Well over a decade ago, Cochran-Smith and Fries's seminal paper provided a clear delineation of the two key battle lines in the teacher education debate which was sweeping across the US:

the agenda to professionalize teaching and teacher education … and the movement to deregulate teacher preparation, which aims to dismantle teacher education institutions and break up the monopoly of the profession.

(Cochran-Smith and Fries, 2001, p 3)

The latter is discussed below, and the next chapter seeks to outline an ideal type of professional.

It has taken around 10 years for the former to reach England where the deregulation agenda has been moved forward through the reinstitution of public floggings, disparaging university-based teacher education and its educators as left-wing *'enemies of promise'* (Gove, 2013). Such language may seem somewhat overblown, but the outworking of the recent teacher education reforms in England has had profound and far-reaching impacts, not least in the demise of hundreds of PGCE places and concomitant damage to university education departments (Furlong, 2013). Allied to this is the creation of a multiplicity of competing entrance routes to the profession and government endorsement of the employment of unqualified teachers in the increasing number of academies and free schools across England. It is notable that similar changes have not happened in other parts of the UK where, by contrast, teacher and teacher educator professionalisation agendas are being pursued (The Teacher Education Group, 2015).

Finally, perhaps there should be an important contemporary yet perennial addition to the exemplars within this quadrant. The de-professionalised quadrant may also be considered the locus of those migrant and refugee teachers who find that their previous qualifications and experience count for little in their new state even though that state may have teacher shortages which may be exacerbated by the arrival of immigrants and refugees (Penson and Yonemura, 2012). Restoring these teachers to the equivalent of their former professional status is likely to entail some specialist CPD.

The 'dragons' fight back

The much derided senior teacher education academics in England have fought back against this neoliberal tide, most significantly in Furlong's book, *Education: The Anatomy of the Discipline*, which is tellingly sub-titled *Rescuing the University Project* (2013). In addition, Furlong and colleagues sought to delineate and champion the distinctive strengths of university-based teacher education by bringing together the British Educational Research Association and the Royal Society of Arts jointly to sponsor the UK-wide *Inquiry into the Role of Research in Teacher Education* (BERA-RSA, 2014) which is discussed in the next chapter. In the US, such public castigation of the profession has been characterised and critiqued as part of wider long-standing *'teacher wars'* by Goldstein (2014), while Dingwall and Hillier (2015) present the public blaming of teachers (and other professionals) for systemic failures as *blamestorming*.

This book, like others in the series, seeks to support the development of a well-informed and thoughtful profession. Such support is becoming an ever more important consideration in those places where, as MacBeath (2012) suggests, school-based teacher education routes mean that new teachers can become

captives of the physical, ideological and curricular structures to which they are introduced in induction programmes which bypass colleges and universities with their 'tiresome' theories, disciplinary knowledge and academic 'conceits'.

(MacBeath, 2012, p 97)

Alternatively, university education departments should offer student teachers research-based evidence and intellectual challenge, because *without exposure to alternative insights into what it means to be a professional educator in a changing world, there is less and less opportunity for the future to exist in the present.*

(MacBeath, 2012, p 97)

IN A **NUTSHELL**

This quadrant may be seen as merely an infrequently visited, weed-strewn detour on a career-long professional learning trajectory. However, it is an important byway, not least because of the impact of the deriders and the derided on learners, on individual student teachers and on the profession more widely. Student teachers need to be forewarned of these impacts and their causes, both locally and globally, lest they risk becoming de-professionalised themselves. There has always been an extent to which teachers reflect the wider values of society, but the leading professional actors must seek to inform and shape those values even while being informed and shaped themselves. The next chapter seeks to examine what it means to be the epitome of a professional teacher.

REFLECTIONS ON **CRITICAL ISSUES**

Most people have been to school, have spent hours observing the work of teachers and may well have come to the conclusion that this is easy work which can and should be readily appraised by virtually anyone. The teaching profession and individual teachers need to be able to respond to such critiques, and student teachers, in particular, may need more resilient supporters to come to their defence in private and in public, especially where the critics are speaking from positions of considerable power. Meanwhile, some members of the profession itself may feel it necessary to join the chorus of negativity and sarcasm which is often present in at least one corner of every staffroom. Student teachers can be easy targets, and cynicism may increase in volume and duration as teachers are increasingly forced to work for longer before having access to pension funds. These are very real dangers for the profession and for individual teachers. They require concerted, research-backed strategies and tactics.

Further reading

TES advice on classroom cynics. Available at: http://newteachers.tes.co.uk/news/dealing-colleagues-how-handle-cynics-staffroom/23169 (accessed 9 September 2015), and a positive antidote in *A Passion for Teaching* by Christopher Day (2004).

Cochran-Smith, M and Fries, M K (2001) Sticks, Stones, and Ideology: The Discourse of Reform in Teacher Education. *Educational Researcher*, 30(8): 3–15. [online] Available at: www.udel.edu/educ/whitson/897s05/files/ER-SticksStones.pdf (accessed 9 September 2015).

Paper is freely available online and clearly lays out the origins and nature of the arguments on either side of the teacher education debate.

- *Who are your global education heroes? Describe the teacher who you think should occupy the top right of the Place Model. What are the distinctive characteristics of the consummately professional teacher?*
- *How important is it to develop a Masters-level research-based teaching profession?*
- *How important is teachers' subject knowledge in an age of ambient information?*

Introduction

There is little agreement as to what constitutes an ideal teacher, and in addition, as Thomas (2013) points out, there is also a surprising gap in the public's knowledge of even the most distinguished educationalists who have shaped either the discipline of education or the practice of the teacher. Thus far, this book's account of the Place Model (see page x) has largely pointed towards what an ideal teacher *is not*. It seems incomprehensible that those in charge of any education system would have ambitions for anything less than an ideal and to ensure that those who seek to lead, to teach, to mentor and to inspect teachers are inhabitants of this quadrant. An examination of the other quadrants of the Place Model, however, points to less perfect realities.

So, perhaps, it is best to start at the destination by proffering one ideal type of teacher and, by way of contrast, the restricted local heroes of the proto-professional quadrant (Chapter 2), by considering some of the global heroes who might populate the professional quadrant. You will recall that this book had its starting point in the work of Eric Hoyle, who contrasted the narrow focus of the restricted professional with that of the extended professional:

An extended professional was construed as a teacher for whom teaching was a rational activity, who sought to improve practice through reading, and through engaging in continuous professional development, who was happily collegial, and who located classroom practice within a larger social framework.

(Hoyle, 2008, p 291)

The restricted-extended continuum is the basis of the horizontal axis of the model which is conceptualised as an expanding place, a cumulative, career-long professional learning journey from local to global. This chapter seeks to define the *extended* end of this continuum by drawing on the international literature expertise base to delimit and exemplify the basic characteristics of one ideal professional for the early twenty-first century. As teacher educators, we must then stand back and allow each student teacher to critique this ideal for themselves. The starting point of the chapter is this very autonomy which must underpin professionalism, together with the accountability which is its necessary counterbalance: 'a professional both acts wisely and can explain his or her actions' (Shulman, 1999, p xiii). It is contended that, in addition, teachers must at a minimum be well-qualified, career-long learners (of subjects, of pedagogical content knowledge [PCK], of professional values and practice, and of many other things besides), engage in critical reflection and be evidence-based practitioners, connecting to the best of what is known globally about all aspects of learning and teaching.

In order to complete their consideration of this quadrant, you should then ask students to consider how the ideal compares to reality, in the form of their own educational heroes and of an exemplar drawn from the UK finalists of the Global Teacher Prize (Varkey Foundation, no date), a US$ one million award which was avowedly created in order to improve the status of teachers. While this Prize sits oddly within the usual rubrics of the profession (its celebration of celebrity might be seen by some as the antithesis of professionalism), it does recognise a perceived need to publically acknowledge and substantially reward the achievements and leadership of the most accomplished members of the profession.

Autonomy and accountability

In Chapter 1 it was asserted that student teachers must, first and foremost, be disabused of any illusions they may have that their education system is either designed or equipped to turn them into the very best teacher they can be. They must do this for themselves. There will, of course, be support and advice available, to a greater or lesser extent. Their initial teacher education course should provide a firm foundation, but the autonomy which is necessary to sustain a cumulative, career-long learning trajectory and to seek to attain and maintain the highest professional status is the bedrock of what it means to be a professional.

It has been suggested that government-driven accountability and marketisation agendas have damaged the professional autonomy of teachers (Evans, 2008, p 20; Hoyle and Wallace, 2005, p 100). This is most evident in respect of increasing public emphasis on robust inspection regimes, statutory school curricula (which increasingly define both content and pedagogy), school league tables, micromanagement, rigidly defined targets and the Value-Added Methods that judge teachers by their pupils' grades. The tensions between policy prescription and teacher autonomy, and between teacher autonomy and teacher accountability, are both important and perpetual. While being autonomous professionals, teachers must, nonetheless, accept policy guidance and the necessity of accountability. It would be useful for your students to consider to whom teachers are accountable. Perhaps, they might begin by making a (very long) list and decide whether the profession itself should come top of that list.

Additionally, your students must consider whether being autonomous is so important that teachers without autonomy cease to be professionals and are de facto confined to the proto-professional quadrant of the Place Model as technicists, craftworkers and deliverologists, following procedural guidelines to deliver the ideas of others to learners (Chapter 2). The Place Model also points to a potential susceptibility, in an age of ambient information, to being replaced by robots – let us not forget Arthur C. Clarke's warning (Chapter 3) that '*any teacher who can be replaced by a robot should be*' (1980, p 96). The ideal professional should be able to argue that their role is too complex – too open to innovation, creativity, ambiguity and risk – to be done by robots. They are autonomous, not automatons.

From learner-teachers to teacher-learners

A key reason why teaching is regarded as a profession is the protean complexity of the work which requires sophisticated sets of knowledge, understanding and skills. A teacher's career-long learning journey must involve moving from being learner-teachers to being teacher-learners, becoming more competent and confident teachers while also engaging in the learning needed to enhance their teaching and their career progression. There is considerable agreement with the notion that teachers must be learners throughout their careers (Darling-Hammond and Sykes, 1999), but there is less agreement on what type of learning is best and how it is to be organised, structured, funded and accredited. The tensions between autonomy and accountability can be played out in respect of each of these factors and also in the essential decisions as to what is to be learned and to what standard.

We have come to understand that teachers are professionals precisely because they operate under conditions of inherent novelty, uncertainty and chance. Although there may be curricula that strive to prescribe teacher behaviours with great precision, for most teachers a typical day is fraught with surprises. This is the case for most other professionals – physicians, attorneys, journalists, social workers and others. Therefore, their work cannot be controlled by rules although it must be governed by standards.

(Shulman, 1999, p xiii)

There is no international agreement as to the fundamentals of initial teacher education, although in many countries lists of basic standards and/or competencies have been developed. As autonomous professionals, teachers should also set their own standards and seek to improve their own competences. Other books in this series explore the nature of professional learning more fully (Burn et al, 2014; Philpott, 2014), so the following section provides only outlines of some of the most essential elements of learning which can contribute to creating an ideal teacher. It is recognised, however, that the individual learning needs of teachers will vary considerably between teaching contexts and across a teacher's career.

Subject expertise

It seems axiomatic that teachers must be well-educated and enthusiastic experts in the subject content they teach and must update this knowledge throughout their careers. In some parts of the world, though, either because of the resource-poor expediency of some of the poorest nations or based on political ideology in some of the wealthiest nations, there are many unqualified teachers teaching learners in the early twenty-first century.

In England, since 2012 (Department for Education, 27 July 2012a), the rapidly growing number of academies have had the same freedom as free schools and independent schools to employ teachers who do not have either a teaching qualification or a degree in their specialist subject. The narrowness of focus of subject specialism has also been questioned at a time when there is increasing emphasis in many national curricula on interdisciplinary learning, which can enable both teachers and learners to broaden and deepen their understanding through exploring links across subject boundaries. It is notable, however, that the Conservative government minister who sanctioned the spread of unqualified teachers in England is a staunch champion of discrete subject knowledge. This ensured that the revised statutory national curriculum (Department for Education, 2014) has a strong emphasis on subject content and on pupils learning by rote – for example, large chunks of Shakespearan plays in English, the names of kings and queens in history and the capital cities in geography. The latest review of teacher education in England, likewise, emphasises the importance of *subject knowledge development during initial teacher training* (Carter, 2015, p 67). Subject and interdisciplinary approaches are not, however, incompatible. Indeed, it may be argued that secure subject knowledge provides a firm foundation for interdisciplinary teaching and learning.

Pedagogical content knowledge

The Welsh government's review of the curriculum and assessment, led by Professor Graham Donaldson (2015), noted a need for high-quality teachers with a sound understanding of the *why* and *how* of teaching as well as the *what* (p 58). This is very much in keeping with a growing recognition of the need for teachers to supplement secure subject knowledge with PCK. It is recognised that this is a *slippery term* (Van Driel et al, 2001, p 984), but it is well summed up, elsewhere in this series, as *the knowledge skilled teachers have that allows them to understand their subject in ways that make it teachable* (Philpott, 2014, p 23). Understanding of PCK is as yet most fully developed in science subjects but is increasingly a salient component of teacher education in both higher education and school contexts. It is helpful for students to differentiate this important element of their professional expertise and learning, not least because it is confidence in PCK which will allow them to bring subjects to life in the classroom. Confident PCK draws upon and builds secure subject knowledge and also connects an individual teacher's classroom to the latest global research, as discussed below.

In the UK, subject associations play an increasingly strong role in independently supporting subject teachers to keep abreast of both subject and PCK innovation and in robustly defending the place of their subject in the curriculum – for example, at times of curriculum review, when subjects may be under threat. Your students might benefit from being asked to find out more about the support offered by their subject associations. Public examination bodies, too, increasingly provide CPD and subject resources, but these can have a strong technicist focus, supporting teaching to the test, an approach which is reinforced by comparative school league tables. This latter point highlights one of the many matters which call upon a teacher's understanding of professional values.

Professional values

Hargreaves and Fullan (2012, p 5) assert that a teacher who is professional will still be professional '*even when no one is looking*'. Teaching can be an isolated occupation, and a teacher facing professional dilemmas, either alone or with colleagues, needs to be able to draw on a value base which, at the very least, points them away from unprofessionalism, as discussed in Chapter 4 which underscored the need to codify and enforce professional behaviour, rooted in clearly stated professional values. This is often the province of a professional body such as the 'General Teaching Council' or a 'College of Teaching'. The development of the latter has been mooted in England (DfE, 2014), but the closure of the College of Social Work in June 2015 does not bode well for this important proposition.

A recent UNESCO and IIEP (Van Nuland, 2008, p 7) report underlines the need for '*the collective conscience of the profession*' to regulate the behaviour of its members. Chapter 4 examined some examples of unprofessional behaviour and presented the somewhat skeletal, but accessible, GTCNI *Code of Values* (GTCNI, 2007). This chapter, seeking to identify an ideal, asks if it might be beneficial for every teacher to connect with such values by swearing a professional oath, akin to that in Singapore, where newly qualified teachers are also presented with a symbolic compass to show them the right direction. The Labour opposition in Britain, in 2012, proposed that a similar process be adopted. It was greeted with some scorn by Conservative ministers and also by teachers themselves on Twitter, with the latter (perhaps predictably) inventing a range of more irreverent oaths:

» *I pledge that I will leave this demoralised profession as a bitter and burnt-out shell at the earliest opportunity.*

» *I pledge to work 60 hour weeks before I'm forced out with complete exhaustion.*

» *I pledge not to cry and hide in my cupboard when things start going wrong, and to always refill the staff room kettle if empty.*

» *I promise to nod sagely at every new and time-consuming initiative that will undoubtedly be reversed in 18 months' time.*

» *I swear to follow education policies thought up by people with no relevant experience apart from the fact they went to school.*

(*The Daily Telegraph*, 2014)

It is widely believed that medical doctors still swear the Hippocratic Oath. In fact, it is not compulsory, but some medical schools now hold a ceremony where graduating doctors do swear an updated version of the oath. The General Medical Council (GMC) has drafted a new version of the Oath on behalf of the World Medical Association, which your student teachers might usefully consider redrafting for the teaching profession (www.patient.co.uk, no date).

In concluding this section, you should note that there are many, many other areas of expertise which fall within the remit of an ideal teacher. Lists of teaching standards or competences seek comprehensively to define and to delimit such matters, but even the most cursory exploration of classroom management – or pastoral care, for example – highlights the enormity and complexity of these areas alone. In addition to ensuring a secure and ongoing development of the relevant knowledge, understanding and skills, there has, for the past 50 years, been an increasing acceptance that the best way to deal with such complexity is through adopting *critical reflection* as a key component of the cumulative, career-long professional learning journey.

Reflective teachers

The exploration of reflection in this chapter, firstly, uses an example drawn from popular literature, in keeping with the use of literature in some earlier chapters to stimulate debate, and, secondly, highlights the global, profession-wide potential of reflective teaching.

Watton and colleagues (2001) use this extract from the novel *Harry Potter and the Goblet of Fire* to describe reflection. In this extract, Dumbledore, the head teacher of Hogwarts School, is speaking to his pupil wizard Harry Potter about having excess thoughts:

Harry stared at the stone basin. The contents had returned to their original, silvery white state, swirling and rippling beneath his gaze. 'What is it?' Harry asked shakily. 'This? It is called a Pensieve', said Dumbledore. 'I sometimes find, and I am sure you know the feeling, that I simply have too many thoughts and memories crammed into my mind.' 'Err', said Harry who couldn't truthfully say that he had ever felt anything of the sort. 'At these times' said Dumbledore, indicating the stone basin, 'I use the Penseive. One simply siphons the excess thoughts from one's mind, pours them into a basin, and examines them at one's leisure. It becomes easier to spot patterns and links, you understand, when they are in this form.'

(Rowling, 2000, pp 518–19)

Moreover, Watton and colleagues (2001) note that '*like many of Rowling's invented terms, Pensieve*' is a portmanteau term, combining the words '*pensive*' and '*sieve*'. The latter is an object in which something may be sorted, drained or separated, and *Pensive* is derived from the Latin *pensare*, meaning *to ponder*. Thus, a *pensieve* allows for the careful sorting of thoughts or memories. Small groups of students might be asked to devise a virtual pensieve into which they might pour the most uncomfortable moment in their teaching practice to date, to discuss how they dealt with the moment and how, on reflection, they *could have* dealt with it.

The skills required for reflective teaching are comprehensively discussed elsewhere (Pollard et al, 2008), but it is very important to point out that not all thinking about teaching constitutes reflective teaching. Zeichner and Liston (2014) draw a contrast between technical teaching (as in the proto-professional quadrant; Chapter 2) and reflective teaching:

If a teacher never questions the goals and the values that guide his or her work, never considers the context in which he or she teaches, or never examines his or her assumptions, then it is our belief that this individual is not engaged in reflective teaching.

(Zeichner and Liston, 2014, p 1)

Reflective teachers are capable of critiquing both their own values and their own professional contexts. Donaldson, in his report on the review of teacher education in Scotland, describes the potential global range of reflective practice by outlining a model of a teacher who:

is the kind of professional who is highly proficient in the classroom and who is also reflective and enquiring not only about teaching and learning, but also about those wider issues which set the context for what should be taught and why ... This concept of professionalism takes each individual teacher's responsibility beyond the individual classroom outwards into the school, to teacher education and the profession as a whole.

(Donaldson, 2010, p 15)

In this global context, an important question might be posed linking the professional quadrant to the *no teacher* segment of the Place Model. The GMC, in their good practice guidance, sets out that it is a doctor's duty to offer help if an emergency arises (while also taking into account their own safety, competence and availability for other opportunities of care). Your students might be asked to consider whether teachers should have a wider moral duty towards those many millions of learners who have no teachers. The General Teaching Council for Northern Ireland's (GTCNI) *Code of Values* (2007) suggests that:

teachers will at all times be conscious of their responsibilities to others: learners, colleagues and indeed the profession itself.

(GTCNI, 2007, p 3)

This is a global moral challenge worthy of consideration by the global professionals of this quadrant. The following section also presents a further significant global challenge, that of connecting local practice to the global research base of education.

Evidence-based practitioners

David Hargreaves's speech to the Teacher Training Agency (1996) is widely credited as a key impetus for evidence-based practice in education. Hargreaves accused educational research of not having generated the cumulative body of relevant knowledge that would enable teaching to become a research-based profession, while Biesta in 2007 looked back to Hargreaves, noting some progress, but berated a narrow and '*undemocratic*' focus only on '*what works*'. Menter (2011) argues that there is little research-based evidence about teacher professional development itself:

Considering how ubiquitous the practice of professional education for teachers is within schools and departments of education in universities across the world, it is surprising how relatively under-developed it is as a field of research.

(Menter, 2011, p 11)

Nonetheless, teachers are exhorted to engage with research in practice in order to improve their own practice (Goldacre, 2013), while teacher educators are encouraged to help student teachers to become both critical consumers and competent producers of research. Further, Nelson and O'Beirne's (2014) literature review for the National Foundation for Education Research (NFER) suggests that too little is known about the efficacy of evidence-based practice in education and calls for government support for the development of an infrastructure to support and disseminate educational research.

Thus, in recent years we have witnessed a spiral of cannibalistic confrontation which looks something like this: educationists tell government minsters that their education policies are not evidence-based while being forced to admit that their assertion that evidence-based practice is effective is not itself evidence-based, even while adding a triumphalist (but futile) coda which points a reprimanding finger at government for underfunding educational research, while, in response, ministers pour scorn on the quality of educational research ...

This surreal scenario is acknowledged by the recent *Inquiry into Research in Teacher Education* (BERA-RSA, 2014), which might itself be seen as a somewhat belated reaction to the expansion of school-based teacher education and unqualified teachers in England. Nonetheless, the *Inquiry* served the purpose of drawing on expertise from across the globe to produce the eloquent and structured arguments which have, for too long, been missing from this important component of teacher professionalism. It is an issue which harks back over 30 years to Hoyle's paradox (1983) which was the starting point of this book, namely that teachers are seeking to be recognised as professionals while undertaking the sorts of CPD which will not further that cause. Progress has been too slow, and only some education systems have bought into research-based teacher education by introducing Masters-level courses. Exceptionally, the entry requirement for permanent employment as a teacher in all Finnish basic and high schools today is a Masters degree, and Masters ITE courses have recently been introduced in other countries including Portugal and Ireland. Watson and Drew (2015) suggest that universities seek to construct a desire for career-long professional learning which emphasises the criticality and masterliness which can be accredited within their frameworks. The profession must consider the potential intrinsic and extrinsic value of these offerings: providing useful learning while also enhancing the status of the profession.

In other professions, meanwhile, Masters-level CPD has been a long-standing feature, and full-time practitioner-researchers are employed in professions such as nursing where the researcher is often shared across groups of hospitals and other healthcare providers. Student teachers might be asked to review the final report of the *Inquiry* (BERA-RSA, 2014) and to consider the job description for a teacher-researcher which would include supporting student teachers with their practice-based research across a group/consortium/chain of schools, colleges and other education providers.

The remainder of this chapter exemplifies those who might putatively populate this section of the Place Model. Of course, it might be argued (I hope!) that very many experienced teachers would fit themselves somewhere in the sector together with all inspectors, teacher educators and CPD providers.

Global educational heroes

This section provides details of two educational heroes and invites you to judge the appropriateness of the examples. The first is known to the author, in a professional capacity; the second is drawn from a recently instigated global competition which aimed to draw the world's attention to the best teachers.

Professor David Lambert

The Geographical Association's Chief Executive, David Lambert, who is Chair of Geography Education at University College London (UCL) describes his professional profile as follows:

I was a comprehensive school geography teacher for 12 years, becoming a Deputy Headteacher in 1985. I joined the Institute of Education (IoE) in 1986–7 as a teacher educator, becoming Reader in Education in 1999 and enjoying a spell as Assistant Dean ITE (research). I played a leading role in introducing the Master of Teaching (MTeach) at the Institute. In 2002 I left the IoE to became full-time Chief Executive of the Geographical Association, helping to guide its transformation into a significant provider of CPD and a leader in funded curriculum development activity. From September 2007 I had the opportunity to combine this role with a return to the IoE as Professor of Geography Education. Recent publications include 'Geography 11–19: a conceptual approach', co-written with John Morgan. My overarching goal is to advance the importance of geography in schools, not least its role in helping young people grasp the significance of the Anthropocene.

(Institute of Education, no date)

An additional piece of evidence to support his positioning in the quadrant is that Lambert hosts an impressive blog. This includes an interesting discussion of the debate about the *knowledge turn* in the curriculum, including his tongue-in-cheek response to the assertion by a junior minister, based on the claims of a key government adviser, that pupils '*must know the rivers of England*'. Lambert's response, '*What, all of them?*' (Institute of Education, no date), met with immediate admonishment from the minister and is now the stuff of geography educators' folklore. His more serious point was, of course, '*how many of the rivers of England would constitute a pass mark and even more seriously: what do we mean by "know"?*' (Institute of Education, no date).

The Global Teacher Prize (introduced in 2014 by the Varkey Foundation) was ostensibly aimed at improving teacher status because '*the status of teachers in our cultures is key to our global future*' (Varkey, 2014). The Prize, which is described as the 'Nobel Prize' of teaching, operates under the patronage of His Highness Sheikh Mohammed bin Rashid Al Maktoum, UAE vice president, prime minister and ruler of Dubai, and offers an annual award of one million US dollars. The second example of an educational hero is a UK science teacher shortlisted for the Prize in 2014.

Dr Richard Spencer

Middlesbrough College, Billingham, United Kingdom

Richard first completed a PhD in molecular biology and became a post-doctoral researcher and then trained as a teacher. His approach to teaching 16 to 18 year-olds A-level biology involves as much variety as possible to make lessons interesting, engaging and memorable. He uses experiments, fieldwork, videos, e-learning, models, role play, simulations, analogies, learning games – and the occasional poem, song and dance. He has found that performing biology songs and dances helps his students remember complicated biological processes and learn numerous new terms.

Richard has won several teaching awards, including the Salters Prize for Teaching Chemistry and two national STAR awards (Further Education Teacher of The Year and Outstanding Subject Learning Coach). He led his biology department to win a UK National Association of Colleges Beacon Award for Excellence in Teaching and Student Achievement in Biology. He was awarded Chartered Science Teacher status by the Association of Science Education & Science Council UK (2007) and Chartered Biologist status by the Society of Biology (2013). Richard was appointed Member of the British Empire (MBE) in the New Year's Honours List (2010) for services to science communication and was named as one of the UK's Top 100 Practising Scientists in 2014.

He has contributed to a long list of national and international conferences and teacher training workshops. Richard has also provided numerous online resources for teachers as well as award-winning e-learning courses for students. Locally he has taken part in several initiatives that aim to generate enthusiasm for science in school children. He also implemented a highly successful before-school literacy program called 'Breakfast with Books' that increased academic achievement of ethnic minority and at-risk students.

If awarded the Prize, Richard would like to use some of the funds to enable him to condense his full-time teaching into three or four days per week. This would allow him to work on projects, visit schools and colleges and develop other teachers pro bono during the rest of the week. He would also support a project run by The Research Foundation to Cure AIDS that aims to write a science opera on AIDS and HIV in order to raise general awareness of the ongoing threat posed by this dangerous virus.

(Varkey Foundation)

Ask your student teachers to compare these profiles with the qualities of a highly professional teacher as described in this chapter and with the teacher heroes whom they would nominate to populate this quadrant of the Place Model.

IN A **NUTSHELL**

This chapter provides a conception of an ideal teacher and proffers some examples for discussion. The listing of key qualities cannot be exhaustive, but certainly provides an outline of the most necessary features of those who might occupy this quadrant of the Place Model. It offers both a signpost and a target for new entrants to the profession and also a pedestal on which a high-status teacher might be both acclaimed and derided. This sector of the Model is home to the profession's standard bearers, pioneers, leaders, appraisers and heroes.

REFLECTIONS ON **CRITICAL ISSUES**

The chapter confronts the profession's naysayers by constructing an ideal teacher as an autonomous, accountable, reflective, evidence-based and career-long learner. Confident, up-to-date expertise in subjects and in the PCK which is required to teach them effectively will still feature as important priorities even in an age of freely available ambient information. The lower status quadrants of the Place Model demonstrate amply the importance of critical reflection and a professional value base against which teachers can be held accountable to their learners and to the society more widely.

Further reading

Pollard, A, Anderson, J, Maddock, M, Swaffield, S, Warin, J and Warwick, P (2008) *Reflective Teaching – Evidence-Informed Professional Practice*, 3rd edition. London: Continuum. [online] Available at: www.freerangeproduction.com/Reflective%20Teaching.pdf (accessed 9 September 2015).

CRITICAL **ISSUES**

- *What is the point of low-status, learning-limited, short-term teachers?*
- *What is the point of teachers who are unable to define, assert, enhance and police their professionalism both individually and collectively, locally and globally?*

Introduction

This book began with a paradox, defined by Hoyle in 1983, the year in which the author became a teacher. Responding to the question, 'Is teaching a profession?', Hoyle argued that teachers were seeking professional recognition, but were not engaging in the sorts of professional development which would enhance their professional status. Hoyle's paradox still exists. Burstow and Maguire (2014), aiming to *'disentangle what it means to be a teacher in the twenty-first century'*, contend that *'there is confusion about teachers' place in society'* and that *'in continuing professional learning the emphasis lies with success in school experience and technical skills'*. They argue for an increased recognition of the importance of *'other equally important aspects of teachers' professional learning ... commitment, values, judgement ... and ... for teachers becoming "agents of change" and in control of their professional destinies'* (Burstow and Maguire, 2014, p 117).

The pessimist would suggest that the teaching profession has missed opportunities to better delineate, maintain and communicate its destiny, its external thresholds and internal values, its distinctive ideals and frailties and its singular place in the world. It is, therefore, more vulnerable to an erosion of status, which has resonances with Hoyle's paradox at its core and which benefits no one, neither teachers nor learners. The challenges for the profession must also be set in the wider societal context of the need to counterbalance the overadjustments of postmodernism, which have cast aside professional authority with too great an alacrity. There is a need to rebuild the teaching profession for a new century in which learners still need learned, versatile and confident professionals, even while retaining the capacity to question their authority.

The optimist would seek a positive and forward-looking response to Hoyle's persistent paradox. This book provides a constructive and original vision which is based around an innovative model of teacher professionalism, the Place Model. The Model utilises two senses of place as the basis for a timely a priori examination of the place of the teacher:

1. place in the sociological sense of hierarchical status; and

2. place in the humanistic geography tradition of place as a cumulative process of professional learning within ever-expanding horizons.

Of course, the Place Model is reductionist and teachers do not have unlimited agency throughout either of these places. Nonetheless, using these two senses of place yields a thought-provoking set of perspectives on the teaching profession. The chapters of the book present and putatively populate a range of *places* for the profession, current and historic, fictional and real. In doing so, the Model poses important questions about teachers on behalf of learners everywhere. This final chapter uses the Place Model to underscore the ways in which, firstly, the profession as a whole and, secondly, individual teachers can endeavour to provide the best possible teaching for every learner on the planet.

Lessons for the profession

It is important not to overlook the *elephant* in the model, the iniquitous global teacher shortage, as discussed in Chapter 3 but rarely debated by the profession as a whole. The twenty-first-century world is one in which both endemic poverty and episodic disasters mean that every day there are millions of learners who do not have a chance to attend school. In the poorest parts of the world, even where some teachers are available, they are too often overstretched but also underqualified and/or poorly behaved (Chapter 4). Nor are such teachers confined to the most destitute corners of the planet, and everywhere their impact is far from benign, for both individuals and nations. Even where they are well-qualified and faultlessly behaved, teachers may not be willing to stay in teaching when higher status occupations offering better chances of career-long learning beckon. Dealing with such precarious teachers is set to be a strong focus of the post-Millennium Development Goals agenda. This imperative can be supported by the work of professional bodies which, where they exist and where they have capacity (funding, status, rigour, ambition ...), are increasingly prepared to define, disseminate and police professional standards:

Perhaps the central challenge for educators is whether they can create means for self regulation that are sufficiently robust that they will inspire public confidence in the process

(Darling-Hammond and Liebermann, 2012, p 169)

The establishment of internationally agreed-upon standards for qualified teacher status seems to be an obvious, if enormously challenging, first step. An even greater test is posed around developing a shared conception of how the learner-teacher might be best supported throughout a compulsory, yet individualised, career-long journey as a teacher-learner. As working years increase, the importance of sustained and sustaining career-long learning journeys also increases. It is ever more important that this journey should avoid the technicism, craftworking and *deliverology* of the proto-professional (Chapter 2), uncritically replicated across the years. It must also circumvent internally or externally driven de-professionalisation (Chapter 5). Internal cynicism and external derision can poison individual careers and public perceptions of teachers. Nonetheless, as has been demonstrated most recently in England, politically driven attacks on the profession can have remarkably positive consequences when they spur the most senior members of the profession to engage in both critical reflection and in outstanding acts of valour in the face of the profession's most venomous critics. Both learners and learner-teachers deserve to be protected from the most destructive internal and external influencers. New entrants to the profession must also be inoculated with optimism for their future, while the accomplishments of the most accomplished professionals and their positive contributions to the wider profession should be encouraged, acknowledged and rewarded.

Lessons for learner-teachers

This book outlines the optimal type of teaching professional (Chapter 6) and also the most undesirable alternatives (Chapters 2–5). Being encouraged to critically navigate the byways of the Place Model will help to ensure that learner-teachers are forewarned and forearmed in defending themselves and their learners against a range of potential hazards which will surely include:

» attacks from politicians with ideological agendas;

» the latest education fads;

» the attraction of bending the rules in order to look better in league table comparisons;

» silver-tongued purveyors of beguilingly simple recipes for *success* or of the subversion and avoidance of professional duties;

» computerisation of teaching and learning;

» the superficial deliverology of questionable teaching techniques and inadequate *content*; and

» even the complacent temptation to close the blinds, put on a video and snooze while *teaching* Year 10Z on a Friday afternoon.

New entrants to the profession must be critically cognisant of societal and governmental demands. They must also seek to develop the capacity to proactively shape their own career-long professional learning journeys while knowledgably contributing to, and utilising, both local, situated understandings and globally recognised expertise. Only such self-improving teachers are worthy of a place as the high-status teachers who learners everywhere deserve.

Introduction

This workshop is based on the *Living Graph* technique developed by David Leat (1998) as a classroom thinking skills exercise. The technique is intended to help learners to understand graphs by *populating* them with realistic exemplars, flesh and bones, concrete archetypes which bring them to life. Learners work in groups to discuss and debate the selected position of the exemplars and to justify their positioning. In this version of the exercise, the learners may also be challenged to place themselves and other real teachers within the Model.

The tasks

Workshop participants (who might be student teachers, teacher educators or Masters students) will have heard/read a basic explanation of the Place Model (based on Chapter 1) and are given a large preprinted copy of the Model and a number of statements (exemplars such as those shown below) describing a range of different teachers (both fictional and real). The groups are asked to:

1. decide where on the Model these teachers might best be placed. They should be informed that there are no *correct* answers but that they should be able to justify the positions they choose;

2. place themselves on the Model and to place a typical teacher (in their country or local administrative area) in the Model and also to justify these positions;

3. outline the characteristics of an ideal teacher in respect of status (how would high status be evidenced?) and career-long learning.

Debrief discussion and extension activities

Following the group activity, the workshop facilitator conducts a debrief, which is based around asking participants to describe and explain where they have placed each exemplar. The facilitator may choose to add other exemplars, which might have applicability to local issues, or to ask workshop participants to do so.

In addition, as an extension exercise, the groups might each be given one of the critical questions from this book to discuss. Each group leader would then report back to the rest of the group, prompting wider discussion.

A further extension activity might ask participants to imagine that the Place Model could be used to plot a range of professions. Participants might be asked to plot the location of other professions relative to the teaching profession. Other professions might include lawyers, medical doctors, politicians, estate agents, bankers, accountants, dentists, nurses, midwives, social workers, etc.

Exemplar 1

My biggest challenge as a teacher in Uganda is the cost of living. Teachers' salaries in Uganda are very, very low, even when we do get paid, and sometimes the cheques do not arrive, and one of the teachers has to walk to the ministry office in the nearest town to find out why. We either send his class home or take them into our classrooms, which already have around 60 pupils. The pupils are really keen to learn, but it is hard to concentrate when I have so many money worries. I would really like to take part in some continuous professional development to update my skills, especially about how to teach such big classes using active learning.

Exemplar 2

This potential mathematics teacher applicant is from China and has an undergraduate degree in mathematics gained from Guizhi Normal University (an initial teacher training university in China). With a qualified teacher status in China, he had taught mathematics in both secondary and senior high school for nine years before he came to the UK in 2008. He is now living in Scotland and would love to become a mathematics teacher again but has been told that his mathematics teaching qualifications are not acceptable. He has Level 5.5 IELTS – English language qualification (7.5 – suitable for teaching in the UK).

Exemplar 3

I put posters up over the wee window in my classroom door and disappear into my own little empire. We get very bright kids in this school, mostly – a few of them get coached for the entrance exam and shouldn't be here. The rest just need to learn what is in the textbook for the exam and I make sure they do. I had an inspector in my class, observing, the other day. The boss had said the inspectors wanted to see *active learning*, so I did one of those group work, poster-making things. The kids seemed to like it, but one of the brightest whispered to me that I should just dictate the notes as usual. It was a bit of a stage whisper and the inspector overheard. She smiled – I didn't know they could do that – it was unnerving.

Exemplar 4

Joseph is a teacher educator in Malawi. He is currently a Commonwealth fellow at a British university doing a PhD on citizenship education. Citizenship was introduced in the form of a compulsory social studies subject and is examined in junior and senior cycle public exams in Malawi. Joseph has long thought that a *citizenship exam* is an oxymoron and his PhD has convinced him that he is right – but how can he influence policies? Many headteachers and parents think that the more democratic parts of citizenship education have made the pupils more troublesome and more demanding. The school council members have even been monitoring teacher attendance and tardiness in some schools. Joseph had been a geography teacher for eight years. He did a Masters degree at a Norwegian university about 10 years ago and that allowed him to get a job as an inspector. Throughout his career, teaching has never been well paid nor highly esteemed, so he started keeping chickens when he was a teacher and has kept up this sideline – he now employs a former pupil to look after his chicken business, which is thriving.

Exemplar 5

Margaret is a teacher-researcher. She is employed by a university and also by a consortium of 15 schools – 10 primary schools, 1 school for pupils with severe learning difficulties and 4 secondary schools. A local, private, fee-paying school is in the process of joining the consortium and will also be availing of her services. She spends about half of her time in the university and can call upon the assistance of a part-time postdoctoral research assistant. She is expected to publish in peer-reviewed journals and to contribute to the department's research ratings as well as teaching the research component of the postgraduate teacher education course and the Masters in Education. Her favourite part of the job is supporting teachers and student teachers in their small-scale research, but she is most proud of her success in leading a bid for European funding which will allow researchers and teachers to work with partners in two other European countries and in Sri Lanka.

Exemplar 6

John is a recent PGCE graduate in his first teaching post in a local primary school. He has found the first six months distinctly challenging although things are gradually getting better and he is enormously grateful for the help of his mentor, a senior teacher who has shown him the ropes and always been there for a chat at the end of the day. It is early days yet, but he would like to sign up for a Masters and do some classroom-based research to find out more about his pupils' learning, especially in mathematics, which is his forte. He would eventually like to become a numeracy coordinator – he gets the impression that few other teachers have much affinity with mathematics and he thinks that this is a pity, given the subject's importance for everyday life and for all of the other STEM (Science, Technology, Engineering and Mathematics) subjects too.

Exemplar 7

Alicia is a glamorous head of drama in a secondary school. She has been teaching for some 25 years and feels that she knows the job inside-out. Earlier in her career she had thought that she would like to become a senior teacher or vice principal, but when she didn't get the first senior promotion, and her rival did, she found herself gradually slipping into the role of *thorn-in-the-side* of the management, cynic in chief, her sharp tongue and ready wit ensuring she has plenty of *friends*, especially among the female staff. In the drama department, however, she runs a tight ship, tolerating no dissent from her newly qualified assistant teacher and ensuring that she, too, is never too accommodating towards the senior management – being helpfully unhelpful, that's the style!

Exemplar 8

The village all declared how much he knew;
'Twas certain he could write, and cypher too;
Lands he could measure, terms and tides presage,
And ev'n the story ran that he could gauge.
In arguing too, the parson owned his skill,
For even tho' vanquished, he could argue still;
While words of learned length and thundering sound,
Amazed the gazing rustics ranged around;
And still they gazed, and still the wonder grew,
That one small head could carry all he knew.

(Oliver Goldsmith, *The Deserted Village*, 1770)

Exemplar 9

My worst teacher never comes prepared for lessons and hardly ever looks at our work. He comes into class and gives us work to do from the textbook. He shouts at anyone who does not seem to be working and won't answer pupil questions, even when we don't know what we are supposed to be doing. I have learned almost nothing in his class, other than how to keep quiet – or pretend to. He seems to spend his time on the Internet, on Facebook and on Ebay, ordering parts for his motorbikes. I've also started to notice the way he leers at some of the girls – the ones with the shortest skirts – I think he is a creep!

Exemplar 10

I think I have died and gone to heaven! I have just started my first paid teaching post, back in my old primary school – bliss. My dad knows the chair of the board of governors so I think that helped ... they like to bring their *old girls* back as teachers. It seems strange to be working with some of my former teachers, but it is comfortable too. I know where everything is and all the kids' families. I think I just want to settle down and stay here forever.

REFERENCES

ABC News (2013) *Home Schooling German Family Fights Deportation*. [online] Available at: www.abcnews.go.com/US/home-schooling-german-family-fights-deportation/story?id=18842383&page=2 (accessed 9 September 2015).

Acker, S (ed) (1989) *Teachers, Gender and Careers*. New York: Routledge-Falmer Press.

Allen, J and Massey, D (eds) (1995) *Geographical Worlds*. Oxford: Oxford University Press.

Arora, P (2010) Hope-in-the-Wall? A Digital Promise for Free Learning. *British Journal of Educational Technology*, 41(5): 689–702.

Ball, S (2008) *The Education Debate*, 1st edition. Bristol: Policy Press.

Ball, S (2013) *The Education Debate*, 2nd edition. Bristol: Policy Press.

Barmby, P (2006) Improving Teacher Recruitment and Retention: The Importance of Workload and Pupil Behaviour. *Educational Research*, 48: 247–65.

Bayne, S (2015) Teacherbot: Interventions in Automated Teaching. *Teaching in Higher Education*, 20(4): 455–67.

BBC News (2015) 11 Northern Ireland Primary Schools Advised Over Possible Transfer Test Coaching. *BBC News*, 29 January 2015. [online] Available at: www.m.bbc.co.uk/news/uk-northern-ireland-31039169 (accessed 9 September 2015).

Beista, G (2007) Why 'What Works' Won't Work: Evidence-Based Practice and the Democratic Deficit in Educational Research. *Educational Theory*, 57: 1–22.

Bennell, P and Akyeampong, K (2001) *Teacher Motivation in Sub-Saharan Africa and South Asia, Department for International Development (DfID)*. [online] Available at: www.r4d.dfid.gov.uk/PDF/Outputs/PolicyStrategy/ResearchingtheIssuesNo71.pdf (accessed 9 September 2015).

BERA-RSA (2014) *Research and the Teaching Profession Building the Capacity for a Self-Improving Education System, Final Report of the BERA-RSA Inquiry into the Role of Research in Teacher Education*. London: BERA-RSA. [online] Available at: www.bera.ac.uk/wp-content/uploads/2013/12/BERA-RSA-Research-Teaching-Profession-FULL-REPORT-for-web.pdf (accessed 9 September 2015).

Buckler, A (2012) *The Professional Lives of Women Teachers in Sub-Saharan Africa: A Capability Perspective*. Unpublished PhD thesis, The Open University, UK.

Burn, K, Hagger, H and Mutton, T (2014) *Beginning Teachers – Making Experience Count*. Northwich: Critical Publishing.

Burstow, B and Maguire, M (2014) Disentangling What it Means to be a Teacher in the Twenty-First Century: Policy and Practice in Teachers' Continuing Professional Learning, in McNamara, O, Murray, J and Jones, M (eds) *Workplace Learning in Teacher Education: International Practice and Policy*. New York: Springer.

Carter, A (2015) *Carter Review of Initial Teacher Training*. London: Department of Education. [online] Available at: www.gov.uk/government/uploads/system/uploads/attachment_data/file/399957/Carter_Review.pdf (accessed 9 September 2015).

Clarke, AC (1980) Electronic Tutors. *Omni Magazine*, June.

Clarke, L and Abbott, L (2008) Put Posters Over the Glass Bit on the Door and Disappear: Tutor Perspectives on the Use of VLEs to Support Pre-Service Teachers. *Teaching in Higher Education*, 13(2): 169–81.

Clarke, L, Cossa, E, Otaala, J and Kazima, M (2013) *Developing More Effective School and Higher Education Institutional Partnerships*. Paper presented at African Education Week, June 2013, Johannesburg.

Cochran-Smith, M and Fries, M K (2001) Sticks, Stones, and Ideology: The Discourse of Reform in Teacher Education. *Educational Researcher*, 30(8): 3–15. [online] Available at: www.udel.edu/educ/whitson/897s05/files/ER-SticksStones.pdf (accessed 9 September 2015).

Commonwealth Secretariat and UNESCO (2011) *Women and the Teaching Profession: Exploring the Feminisation Debate.* [online] Available at: www.unesdoc.unesco.org/images/0021/002122/212200e.pdf (accessed 9 September 2015).

Darling-Hammond, L and Liebermann, A (2012) Teacher Education around the World: What Can We Learn from International Practice? in Darling-Hammond, L and Liebermann, A (eds) *Teacher Education around the World: Changing Policies and Practices.* Abingdon: Routledge, pp 151–69.

Darling-Hammond, L and Sykes, G (eds) (1999) *Teaching as the Learning Profession: A Handbook of Policy and Practice.* San Francisco: Jossey-Bass.

Davies, L (2005) Schools and War: Urgent Agendas for Comparative and International Education. *Compare: A Journal of Comparative and International Education*, 35(4): 357–71.

Davies, L, Harber, C and Schweisfurth, M (2005) *Democratic Professional Development.* Birmingham: CIER/CfBT.

Day, C (2004) *A Passion for Teaching.* London: Routledge-Falmer Press.

Department for Education (2012a) *Academies to Have Same Freedom as Free Schools Over Teachers.* Press Release, 27 July 2012. [online] Available at: www.gov.uk/government/news/academies-to-have-same-freedom-as-free-schools-over-teachers (accessed 9 September 2015).

Department for Education (2012b) *Developing the Teaching Profession to a World Class Standard.* [online] Available at: www.gov.uk/government/consultations/developing-the-teaching-profession-to-a-world-class-standard (accessed 9 September 2015).

Department for Education (2012c) *The National Curriculum, Programmes of Study by Subject.* [online] Available at: www.gov.uk/government/collections/national-curriculum#programmes-of-study-by-subject (accessed 9 September 2015).

Department for Education (2014) *Aspiring to Excellence: Final Report of the International Review Panel on the Structure of Initial Teacher Education in Northern Ireland.* [online] Available at: www.delni.gov.uk/aspiring-to-excellence-review-panel-final-report.pdf (accessed 9 September 2015).

DfID (2013) *Education Position Paper: Improving Learning, Expanding Opportunities.* [online] Available at: www.gov.uk/government/uploads/system/uploads/attachment_data/file/225715/Education_Position_Paper_July_2013.pdf (accessed 9 September 2015).

Dickens, C (1854) *Hard Times.* London: Bradbury and Evans.

Dingwall, G and Hillier, T (2015) *Blamestorming, Blamemongers and Scapegoats: Allocating Blame in the Criminal Justice Process.* Bristol: Policy Press.

Dolton, P and Marcenaro-Gutierrez, O (2013) *Varkey GEMS Foundation Global Teacher Status Index.* London: Varkey. [online] Available at: www.varkeygemsfoundation.org/sites/default/files/documents/2013GlobalTeacherStatusIndex.pdf (accessed 9 September 2015).

Donaldson, G (2010) *Teaching Scotland's Future: Report of a Review of Teacher Education in Scotland.* Edinburgh: The Scottish Government.

Donaldson, G (2015) *The Donaldson Review of Curriculum and Assessment.* Cardiff: The Welsh Government.

Evans, L (2008) Professionalism, Professionality and the Development of Education Professionals. *British Journal of Educational Studies*, 56(1): 20–38.

Frey and Osborne (2013) *The Future of Employment: How Susceptible are Jobs to Computerisation?* Oxford Martin School Working Paper. [online] Available at: www.oxfordmartin.ox.ac.uk/publications/view/1314 (accessed 9 September 2015).

Furlong, J (2013) *Education – An Anatomy of the Discipline: Rescuing the University Project?* Abingdon: Routledge.

Gardiner, P (1995). Teacher Training and Changing Professional Identity in Early Twentieth Century England, *Journal of Education for Teaching*, 21(2): 191–218.

Gates, B (1995) *The Road Ahead*. London: Penguin.

General Medical Council (2013) *Good Practice Guidance*. [online] Available at: www.gmc-uk.org/guidance/good_medical_practice.asp (accessed 9 September 2015).

General Teaching Council for Northern Ireland (2007) *Code of Values and Professional Practice*. [online] Available at: www.gtcni.org.uk/uploads/docs/GTC_code.pdf (accessed 9 September 2015).

General Teaching Council for Scotland (2012) *Code of Professionalism and Conduct (COPAC)*. [online] Available at: www.gtcs.org.uk/standards/copac.aspx (accessed 9 September 2015).

Ginott, H (1972) *The Teacher and the Child*. New York: MacMillan.

Giroux, H (1992). *Border Crossings*. Routledge: London.

Goldacre, B (2013) *Building Evidence into Education*. [online] Available at: www.media.education.gov.uk/assets/files/pdf/b/ben%20goldacre%20paper.pdf (accessed 9 September 2015).

Goldsmith, O (1770) *The Deserted Village*. Dundonald: The Blackstaff Press.

Goldstein, D (2014) *The Teacher Wars: A History of America's Most Embattled Profession*. New York: Random House.

Gove, M (2013) I Refuse to Surrender to the Marxist Teachers Hell-Bent on Destroying Our Schools: Education Secretary Berates 'the New Enemies of Promise' for Opposing his Plans. *Mail on Sunday*, 23 March 2013. [online] Available at: www.dailymail.co.uk/debate/article-2298146/I-refuse-surrender-Marxist-teachers-hell-bent-destroying-schools-Education-Secretary-berates-new-enemies-promise-opposing-plans.html (accessed 9 September 2015).

Grossman, P, Hammerness, K and McDonald, M (2009) Redefining Teacher: Re-Imagining Teacher Education. *Teachers and Teaching: Theory and Practice*, 15(2): 273–90.

Harber, C (2012) Contradictions in Teacher Education and Teacher Professionalism in Sub-Saharan Africa, in R Griffin (ed.) *Teacher Education in Sub-Saharan Africa*. Oxford: Symposium Books.

Harber, C and Davies, L (1997) *School Management and Effectiveness in Developing Countries*. London: Cassell.

Harber, C and Schweisfurth, M (2005) *Democratic Professional Development*. Birmingham: CIER/CfBT.

Harber, C and Stephens, D (2009) *The Quality Education Project: An Evaluation for Save the Children*. Oslo: Save the Children, Norway.

Hargreaves, A and Fullan, M (2012) *Professional Capital: Transforming Teaching in Every School*. New York: Teachers College Press.

Hargreaves, D (1996) *Teaching as a Research-Based Profession: Possibilities and Prospects*. Paper presented at the Teacher Training Agency Annual Lecture, April 1996. [online] Available at: www.eppi.ioe.ac.uk/cms/Portals/0/PDF%20reviews%20and%20summaries/TTA%20Hargreaves%20lecture.pdf (accessed 9 September 2015).

Heaney, S (2012) *Speak the Speech*, speech delivered at the Lyric Theatre, Belfast, (unpublished), 23 May.

Hoyle, E (1983) The Professionalization of Teachers: A Paradox, in Gordon, P (ed) *Is Teaching a Profession?* Bedford Way Papers. London: Institute of Education, University of London.

Hoyle, E (2008) Changing Conceptions of Teaching as a Profession: Personal Reflections, in Johnson, D and Maclean, R (eds) *Teaching: Professionalization, Development and Leadership*. Bonn: Springer, pp 285–304.

Hoyle, E and Wallace, M (2005) *Educational Leadership: Ambiguity, Professionals and Managerialism*. London: Sage.

Ingersoll, R and Strong, M (2011) The Impact of Induction and Mentoring Programs for Beginning Teachers: A Critical Review of the Research. *Review of Educational Research*, 81: 201–33.

Institute of Education (no date) *David Lambert's Blog*. [online] Available at: www.ioelondonblog.wordpress. com/2012/11/27/knowledge-does-not-exist-on-the-internet-it-only-exists-in-the-head (accessed 9 September 2015).

Irish Independent (2014) *Teachers Working for €50 a Week on JobBridge*. [online] Available at: www.independent.ie/irish-news/teachers-working-for-50-a-week-on-jobbridge-29707297.html (accessed 9 September 2015).

Kadzamira, E C (2006) *Teacher Motivation and Incentives in Malawi*. Malawi: University of Malawi.

Kayuni, H and Tambulasi, R (2007) Teacher Turnover in Malawi's Ministry of Education: Realities and Challenges. *International Education Journal*, 8: 89–99.

Kenway, J (1990) Education and the Right's Discursive Politics: Private versus State Schooling, in Ball, S (ed) *Foucault and Education: Disciplines and Knowledge*. London: Routledge, pp 167–206.

Khan Academy. [online] Available at: www.khanacademy.org (accessed 9 September 2015).

Kunzman, R and Gaither, M (2013) Homeschooling: A Comprehensive Survey of the Research. *Other Education: The Journal of Educational Alternatives*, 2(1): 4–59.

Leat, D (ed) (1998) *Thinking through Geography*. Cambridge: Chris Kington Publishing.

Louden, W (2009) 101 Damnations: The Persistence of Criticism and the Absence of Evidence about Teacher Education in Australia. *Teachers and Teaching: Theory and Practice*, 14(4): 357–68.

Lucas, P (1988) Teaching Practice Placements. *British Journal of In-Service Education*, 14(2): 92–99.

MacBeath, J (2012) *Future of the Teaching Profession*, Education International Research Institute, University of Cambridge. [online] Available at: www.download.ei-ie.org/Docs/WebDepot/EI%20Study%20on%20the%20 Future%20of%20Teaching%20Profession.pdf (accessed 9 September 2015).

Maslow, A H (1943) A Theory of Human Motivation. *Psychological Review*, 50: 370–96.

Massey, D (1991) A Global Sense of Place, in Daniels, S and Lee, R (eds) *Exploring Human Geography: A Reader*. London: Arnold, pp 237–45.

McNamara, O and Murray, J (2013) *The School Direct Programme and its Implications for Research-Informed Teacher Education and Teacher Educators*. York: Higher Education Academy.

Menter, I (2011) Teacher Education Research – Past, Present, Future. *BERA Educational Researcher*, 116(Autumn): 11–13.

Menter, I, Hulme, M, Elliot, D and Lewin, J (2010) *Literature Review on Teacher Education in the 21st Century*. Edinburgh: The Scottish Government.

Ministry of Science Education and Technology (MoEST) (2000) *The National Curriculum for Malawi*. Lilongwe: MoEST.

Mitra, S (2012) *Beyond the Hole in the Wall: Discover the Power of Self-Organised Learning*. New York: TED Books.

Mitra, S, Dangwal, R, Chatterjee, S and Jha, S (2005) A Model of How Children Acquire Computing Skills from Hole-in-the-Wall Computers in Public Places. *Information Technologies and International Development Journal*, 2(4): 41–60.

Moon, B and Umar, A (2013) Reorientating the Agenda around Teacher Education and Development, in Moon, B (ed) *Teacher Education and the Challenge of Development*. Abingdon: Routledge, pp 227–39.

Mulkeen, A, Chapman, D and DeJaeghere, J (2007) *Recruiting, Retaining, and Retraining Secondary School Teachers and Principals in Sub-Saharan Africa*. Washington: World Bank Publications.

Murray, J (2002) *Between the Chalkface and the Ivory Towers? A Study of the Professionalism of Teacher Educators Working on Primary Initial Teacher Education Courses in the English University Sector*. Unpublished PhD thesis, Institute of Education, University of London.

NCES (2013) *Digest of Education Statistics*, National Center for Education Statistics. [online] Available at: www.nces.ed.gov/programs/digest/d13/tables/dt13_206.20.asp (accessed 9 September 2015).

Needham, C and Mangan, C (2013) *The Twenty-First Century Public Servant*. Swindon: ESRC. [online] Available at: www.birmingham.ac.uk/Documents/college-social-sciences/public-service-academy/21-century-report-28-10-14.pdf (accessed 21 January 2016).

Nelson, J and O'Beirne, C (2014) *Using Evidence in the Classroom: What Works and Why?* Berkshire: NFER.

OECD (2005) *Teachers Matter: Attracting, Developing and Retaining Effective Teachers*. Paris: OECD.

OECD (2010) *Education at a Glance 2010: OECD Indicators*. Paris: OECD Publishing.

OECD (2011) *Lessons from PISA for the United States: Strong Performers and Successful Reformers in Education*. [online] Available at: www.oecd.org/pisa/46623978.pdf (accessed 9 September 2015).

OECD (2014) *Pisa in Focus, 35*. [online] Available at: www.oecd.org/pisa/pisaproducts/pisainfocus/PISA-in-Focus-n35-(eng)-FINAL.pdf (accessed 9 September 2015).

OFQUAL (2014) *Statistical Release: Malpractice for GCSE and A Level: Summer 2014 Exam Series*. [online] Available at: www.gov.uk/government/uploads/system/uploads/attachment_data/file/386119/malpractice-for-gcse-and-a-level-summer-2014-exam-series.pdf (accessed 9 September 2015).

Patient.co.uk (no date) *Ideals and the Hippocratic Oath*. [online] Available at: www.patient.co.uk/doctor/Ideals-and-the-Hippocratic-Oath.htm (accessed 9 September 2015).

Pension, J and Yonemura, A (eds) (2012) *Next Steps in Managing Teacher Migration: Papers of the Sixth Commonwealth Research Symposium on Teacher Mobility, Recruitment and Migration, Commonwealth Secretariat*. London: UNESCO.

Philpott, C (2014) *Theories of Professional Learning: A Critical Guide for Teacher Educators*. Northwich: Critical Publishing.

Pollard, A (2014) *Reflective Teaching in Schools*. London: Bloomsbury.

Pollard, A, Anderson, J, Maddock, M, Swaffield, S, Warin, J and Warwick, P (2008) *Reflective Teaching: Evidence-Informed Professional Practice*, 3rd edition. London: Continuum.

Pring, R (2012) *The Life and Death of Secondary Education for All*. Abingdon: Routledge.

Public Concern at Work. [online] Available at: www.pcaw.org.uk/schools (accessed 9 September 2015).

Ronfldt, M, Loeb, S and Wyckoff, J (2013) How Teacher Turnover Harms Student Achievement. *American Educational Research Journal*, 50: 4–36.

Rowling, JK (2000) *Harry Potter and the Goblet of Fire*. London: Bloomsbury.

Sahlberg, P (2012) The Most Wanted: Teachers and Teacher Education in Finland, in Darling-Hammond, L and Lieberman, A (eds) *Teacher Education around the World: Changing Policies and Practices*. Abingdon: Routledge, pp 1–21.

Shulman, L (1999) *Foreword to Teaching as the Learning Profession: A Handbook of Policy and Practice*. San Francisco: Jossey-Bass.

Sikes, P (1985) The Life Cycle of the Teacher, in Ball, S and Goodson, I (eds) *Teachers' Lives and Careers*. London: Routledge-Falmer Press, pp 27–60.

Smethem, L (2007) Retention and Intention in Teaching Careers: Will the New Generation Stay? *Teachers and Teaching: Theory and Practice*, 13: 465–80.

Smith, A (2005) Education in the Twenty-First Century: Conflict, Reconstruction and Reconciliation. *Compare*, 35(4): 373–91.

Stockholm International Peace Research institute (SIPIRI) (2015) *Military Expenditure*. [online] Available at: www.sipri.org/research/armaments/milex (accessed 9 September 2015).

Teacher Education Group (2015) *Teacher Education in Times of Change*. Bristol: Policy Press.

Teachers Working Longer Review Group. [online] Available at: www.gov.uk/government/groups/teachers-working-longer-review-group (accessed 9 September 2015).

The Daily Telegraph (2014) *Labour Plan for 'Hippocratic Oath' for Teachers Mocked on Twitter*. 12 October 2014. [online] Available at: www.telegraph.co.uk/education/educationnews/11157045/Labour-plan-for-Hippocratic-oath-for-teachers-mocked-on-Twitter.html (accessed 9 September 2015).

The Guardian (2014) *More than 400,000 Schoolchildren Being Taught by Unqualified Teachers*. 29 December 2014. [online] Available at: www.theguardian.com/education/2014/dec/29/more-than-400000-schoolchildren-taught-unqualified-teachers-tristram-hunt-gove (accessed 9 September 2015).

The Independent (2014) *William Vahey Victims: 'Hundreds' Come Forward to FBI Over Paedophile Teacher Who Taught at London School*. 14 May 2014. [online] Available at: www.independent.co.uk/news/uk/crime/william-vahey-victims-hundreds-come-forward-to-fbi-over-paedophile-teacher-who-taught-at-london-school-9366077.html (accessed 9 September 2015).

Thomas, G (2013) *Education: A Very Short Introduction*. Oxford: Oxford University Press.

Tuan, Y (1977) *Space and Place: The Perspective of Experience*. Minneapolis: University of Minnesota Press.

UNESCO (2009–2014) *Malala: Symbolizing the Right of Girls to Education*. [online] Available at: www.unesco.org/new/en/unesco/resources/malala-symbolizing-the-right-of-girls-to-education/ (accessed 9 September 2015).

UNESCO (2012) *World Atlas of Gender Equality in Education*. [online] Available at: www.unesco.org/new/en/education/themes/leading-the-international-agenda/gender-and-education/ (accessed 9 September 2015).

UNESCO (2014) *Teaching and Learning: Achieving Quality for All, EFA Global Monitoring Report, 2013–2014*. Paris: UNESCO. [online] Available at: www.uis.unesco.org/Library/Documents/gmr-2013-14-teaching-and-learning-education-for-all-2014-en.pdf (accessed 9 September 2015).

UNICEF (2014) *In Sierra Leone, Getting Back to School – on the Airwaves*. [online] Available at: www.unicef.org/infobycountry/sierraleone_76352.html (accessed 9 September 2015).

United Nations (2000) *Millennium Development Goals*. [online] Available at: www.un.org/millenniumgoals/pdf/Goal_2_fs.pdf (accessed 9 September 2015).

United Nations (2013) Secretary-General, at Youth Assembly Featuring Malala Day, Spells Out Biggest Fear of Extremists, Terrorists – 'A Girl with a Book'. Press Release, 12 July 2013. [online] Available at: www.un.org/press/en/2013/sgsm15166.doc.htm (Accessed 9 September 2015).

United Nations Statistics Agency (2013) *Progress towards Universal Primary Education Too Slow*, UIS Newsletter. [online] Available at: www.uis.unesco.org/Education/Documents/fs-25-out-of-school-children-en.pdf (accessed 9 September 2015).

Van Driel, J H, Veal W R and Janessen, F J (2001) Pedagogical Content Knowledge: An Integrated Component within the Knowledge Base for Teaching. *Teaching and Teacher Education*, 17: 979–86.

Van Nuland, S (2009) *Teacher Codes: Learning from Experience*. Paris: UNESCO and IIEP. [online] Available at: www.teachercodes.iiep.unesco.org/teachercodes/resources/Literature_review.pdf (accessed 9 September 2015).

Varkey Foundation (no date) *The Global Teacher Prize*. [online] Available at: www.globalteacherprize.org/about (accessed 9 September 2015).

Washington Post (no date) *Nine Atlanta Educators in Test-Cheating Case are Sentenced to Prison*. [online] Available at: www.washingtonpost.com/local/education/eight-atlanta-educators-in-test-cheating-case-sentenced-to-prison/2015/04/14/08a9d26e-e2bc-11e4-b510-962fcfabc310_story.html (accessed 9 September 2015).

Watson, C and Drew, V (2015) Teachers' Desire for Career-Long Learning: Becoming 'Accomplished' – and Masterly... *British Education Research Journal*, 41(3), 448–461.

Watton, P, Collings, J and Moon, J (2001) *Reflective Writing: Guidance Notes for Students*, Exeter University. [online] Available at: www.exeter.ac.uk/fch/work-experience/reflective-writing-guidance.pdf (accessed 9 September 2015).

Wenger, E (1998) *Communities of Practice: Learning, Meaning, and Identity*. Cambridge: Cambridge University Press.

Winch, C, Oancea, A and Orchard, J (2013) *The Contribution of Educational Research to Teachers' Professional Learning: Philosophical Understandings*. Paper submitted to the BERA-RSA Inquiry. London: BERA/RSA. [online] Available at: www.bera.ac.uk/wp-content/uploads/2014/02/BERA-Paper-3-Philosophical-reflections.pdf?noredirect=1 (accessed 9 September 2015).

World Bank (no date) *The Costs of Attaining the Millennium Development Goals*. [online] Available at: www.worldbank.org/html/extdr/mdgassessment.pdf (accessed 9 September 2015).

Worldmapper (no date) *Girls not in School*, Map No. 201. [online] Available at: www.worldmapper.org/display.php?selected=201 (accessed 9 September 2015).

Wragg, E C (1974) *Teaching Teaching*. Newton Abbot: David and Charles.

Zeichner, K and Liston, D (2014) *Reflective Teaching: An Introduction*, 2nd edition. New York: Routledge.

INDEX